PRAISE FOR CREATIVE CALISTHENICS

"Terri Main knows exactly how to stimulate and motivate a writer.... I am sure Dan Brown could have easily used Main's exercises and created the *DaVinci Code*."

—Lea Schizas
author, *The Muse on Writing*
director, Muse Online Writers' Conference.

"There are a wealth of ideas contained in this small volume and as I was reading I really struggled to resist the urge to quit reading and start writing. This book is a treasure trove of great ideas that will never be far from my desk."

—Len Evans, *Amokarts*
Arts Ministry Outreach for the Kingdom
www.radicallyreal.com

"I know I'm going to keep my copy of Creative Calisthenics close at hand for those days my brain just can't quite get started."

—Penny Lockwood Ehrenkranz
author and freelance writer
in *Vision: A Resource for Writers*
www.lazette.net/Vision

"Creative Calisthenics is a book to sit on top of your Thesaurus—right at your fingertips."

—Kat Crawford,
freelance writer
Straight from the Lion's Mouth

CREATIVE CALISTHENICS

Ultimate Workout for the Writer's Imagination

TERRI MAIN

The Writers' Cafe Press
Indiana

Creative Calisthenics: Ultimate Workout for the Writer's Imagination
Terri Main
Copyright © 2009 by Terri Main

All Rights Reserved.
No parts of this book may be reproduced in any form or by any electronic or mechanical means including information storage and retrieval systems without permission in writing from the publishers, except by a reviewer, who may quote brief passages in a review. For information address The Writers Café Press, P.O. Box 1905, Sumas, WA 98295.

Creative Calisthenics is available with special quantity discounts for bulk purchase for educational needs. Reproducible books or book excerpts can be produced to fulfill special needs. For details, write The Writers Café Press, Special Markets, 101 - 43201 Lougheed Highway, Deroche, B.C. (Canada) V0M 1G0.

The Writers' Café Press
P.O. Box 1905,
Sumas, WA 98295

ISBN: 978-1-934284-11-7

Publisher's Cataloging-in-Publication data

Main, Terri Lynn.
   Creative calisthenics : ultimate workout for the writer's imagination / Terri Main.
   p. cm.
   Includes bibliographical references.
   ISBN 978-1-934284-11-7
1. Authorship. 2. Creative writing. I. Title.

PN145 .M243 2009
808/.02 22—dc22   2009929258

Printed in the United States of America

This book is dedicated to my parents, Justin and Aimee Main, who were always my biggest fans encouraging me in my writing. It is also dedicated to my sister, Tracy Carrisoza. Her love and encouragement kept me going at times when I didn't feel like going on. She also kicked me out of my own house several times so I could complete this volume. If you benefit from the book, you can thank her.

I would also like to acknowledge the encouragement and support of the Fellowship of Christian Writers whose members encouraged me to create this collection.

TABLE OF CONTENTS

Dedication	v
Introduction: A Different Type of Writing Book	xi

TELL ME A STORY
Restoring the Imagination 1

Chance Encounters 2

The Computer Went Crazy and 2

From the Monster's Point of View 3

Magic Doors and Secret Passages 4

The Trunk in the Attic 5

Parables for a New Millenium 5

Only One Day 6

Time Machine 7

Keepsakes 7

Musical Exercises 8

What if . . . ? 9

What Happens Next? 9

JUMPER CABLES FOR THE BRAIN
Rejuvenating Creative Energy 11

Artifacts 11

Ball, Ruler and Hanger 12

More Than One Answer 13

A Funny Thing Happened on the Way to 14

Freewriting 14

Grab Bag 16

Interview of a Lifetime 17

Only $39.95 Plus Shipping and Handling 17

Picture It! 18

Write at First Sight 18

GETTING IDEAS

Replenishing the Idea Barrel 19

Topic Spoking 19

Formula Titles 20

In the Papers 22

In Your Dreams 24

Think Outside the Lyrics: Nonfiction 24

Think Outside the Lyrics: Fiction 25

You Can Quote Me on That 26

Possession of the Good: Nonfiction 27

A Word from Our Sponsor 28

Work a Beat 29

Title Switch 29

OUT AND ABOUT

Stimulation Away From the Computer 31

Ideas in an Art Gallery 31

An Easy Chair and Some Magazines 32

Creativity on the Road 33

Mall Watching 35

What's Down that Road? 36

How'd They Get Here? 37

The Bulletin Board Beat 37

Going on Vacation 38

Stroll Around Town 38

Biographies for Everyone 39

CHARACTERS AND SETTINGS

Developing Memorable Characters and Vivid Settings . . . 41

Background Check 41

Eulogies 42

Home Beautiful 43

Find the Emotion Inside You 44

Help Wanted: Great Characters 44

Award Dinner 45

All the Little People 45

What's on Their Bookshelves 46

Bad Choices 47

Build a Character 47

Favorites 48

Possession of the Good: Fiction 48

I've Got a Secret 50

Send Your Characters Back to School 51

You're the Villain 52

Sick Characters 53

Take Your Main Character to Dinner 54

ORGANIZATION AND PLOTTING
Improving Plots and Outlines 55

Creative Organization 55

Imitate Success 57

I Saw it in the Funny Papers! 59

Special Report 59

Stuck for Ideas? Ask a Character 60

Least Likely 61

Patterns 61

Then the Phone Rang 62

The Worst Thing 62

WAXING POETIC
Using the Example of Poetry Writing 64

Poetry Journal 64

Say Hi to Haiku 65

Sense Poetry 66

Found Poetry 67

WRITING R$_x$
Filling that Blank Screen 69

Answering Your Inner Critic 69

A New Perspective 70

Beat the Clock 72

Cut it in Half 73

Beating the Block 74

Beyond the Visual 76

Hear the Words 77

Twenty-Five Words or Less 78

Video Camera 78

Write a Bad Story 79

Change of Scene 79

GAMES AND COLLABORATIONS
Developing Writing Skills with Others 81

Word Wars 81

"Tag, You're It!" 82

All A-Twitter 83

The Picture Game 84

Get a (Second) Life 84

INTRODUCTION

I've never been an athlete, but, for a short crazy period of my life, I walked in marathons to raise money for the Leukemia and Lymphoma Society. We trained for months for just one marathon. Before each training session, we did stretches. During the week, we did weight training and aerobic exercises. On the weekends, we walked up the side of a mountain (maybe it was a hill, but it felt like a mountain) and down again. Each week we got stronger for the main event – the marathon.

There was no way any of us could wake up one day and say, "Oh, today is the marathon, I'm going to go out and walk or run 26.2 miles." We needed to build up those physical muscles before the marathon. Otherwise, we would never make it to the finish line.

While writing doesn't require the same type of vigorous physical training running a marathon does, it does require a different type of strength. It requires creative strength and a mental flexibility which also comes about through training.

Unlike physical training, which is often boring and painful, training your creative muscles can be fun. That's what this book is all about – pumping up your creativity and having a good time doing so.

A DIFFERENT TYPE OF WRITING BOOK

Most writing books tell you how to write something. They give you information about sentence structure, passive versus active construction, plot elements, characterization, organization, research, writing a query letter and the list goes on.

Creative Calisthenics is different in that we don't tell you how to write. We give you prompts and then we let you write. Using these prompts will help you learn those writing skills, but that is not as important as the fact that they get you writing.

To switch metaphors for a moment, these exercises are jumper cables for the brain. Don't know what to write about today? Flip to any page, and you have an exercise to help you. With over eighty articles detailing more than 175 different exercises, writing prompts, story starters and idea generators, there is always something that can shake loose those mental cobwebs and get you writing.

HOW THIS BOOK CAME ABOUT

I write a column for the Fellowship of Christian Writers email discussion group called "Creative Calisthenics." I post a different exercise or group of exercises each week. Several people suggested they be collected into book form. So, I did. However, I added another twenty essays just for this book.

HOW TO USE THIS BOOK

This is not a book you need to read straight through. In fact, it might be better if you did not. Try opening the book at random and start writing. Let synchronicity be your friend.

The book is loosely organized into chapters. Please, be aware that fitting some of these articles into one chapter or another was challenging because one article often fit under a number of categories. I selected the chapter based on the overall emphasis of the essay.

The chapter divisions can inform your use of this book. Let's say you are having trouble making your main character come alive in your story. Pull an exercise out of the chapter on "Characters and Settings." If your problem is organizing an article, then check out "Organization and Plotting." If you are dealing with writer's block, the section "Jumper Cables for the Brain" is the place to go.

Keep this book handy. It's a small volume. Keep it right on your desk, next to the computer, ready for those times when your creative energy is flagging.

One final note. Don't limit yourself. Don't say, "I'm not a fiction writer, so the section on characterization isn't for me." This isn't about writing your next novel or nonfiction book. It is about stretching and building up those creative muscles. Fiction writers can benefit from the nonfiction exercises, and nonfiction writers can benefit from the fiction prompts. Part of creative muscle building is moving out of the safety of what is familiar and exploring that which is exotic.

I trust this book will be your companion on many enjoyable adventures.

TELL ME
A
STORY

As children we made up fantastic tales about superheroes, knights and princesses, monsters and ballerinas. We pretended to be cowboys and spacemen, doctors and fire fighters, police and criminals. Our stories drove our playtime. As we played, our little imaginations grew.

Somewhere along the way, though, we gave up our permission to pretend. Our education, our work, our "real" life pushed out our imaginary one. We became the teachers, nurses, mechanics, stock brokers, welders, clerks, doctors, lawyers and business executives that our parents and teachers, uncles and aunts, and grandparents expected us to become, and that playful child, full of stories, got lost in a maze of work and responsibility.

Let's find that child.

Today, I give you permission to play "Let's Pretend" and here are a few exercises to get you started.

2   CREATIVE CALISTHENICS

CHANCE ENCOUNTERS

Our lives are filled with "chance" encounters. You decide to go to the gym on Monday instead of Tuesday, and you meet the person who will become your best friend. You go to church one Sunday morning, and you sit behind the person who eventually hires you for your dream job. This exercise is about chance encounters. It is challenging, but my students have a lot of fun with it.

A side note for teachers, "Chance Encounters" makes for a great creative drama group exercise.

This exercise takes some preparation. Get a package of file cards. Pull out about 30-40. On each card, write down a different character. Keep them vague like little girl, sales representative, reporter, actor, starship captain, etc. The more variety you have the better.

After this, take out about 20 cards and write down locations like the supermarket, a space station, street corner, the old west, etc. Again, aim for variety.

Now, comes the fun part. Pull two cards out of the character stack and one card out of the location. Take 15-20 minutes to write a short story or slice of life about these two people meeting in this location. Don't worry if the story is silly (it probably will be) or the writing forced. You are not going to be publishing this. It's just a way to brush away the cobwebs and get started writing.

THE COMPUTER WENT CRAZY AND . . .

We live surrounded by technology. Most of us don't understand any of it or how it works. Sometimes, it seems like it has a mind of its own.

What if it did have a mind of its own? What if one day it had the electronic version of a psychotic break? What would happen? Imagine your computer went crazy (I mean crazier than it already is). What would it do? Would it go on strike and refuse to do any work until you upgraded its memory or bought it a cool new DVD drive? Would it try to take over the world? How might it accomplish these things?

You can do a few variations on this theme. Instead of the computer, imagine your toaster or vacuum cleaner or TV going cra... What if your car went nuts? Okay, it's been done, but your car might go cra... er way. Maybe instead of killing people, she imagines herself to be ...

To see how one poet imagined this scenario ... "Nightmare Number 3" by Stephen Vincent Benet.

FROM THE MONSTER'S POINT OF VIEW

Most of us are familiar with monster movies. They are almost universally told from the monster hunter's perspective. However, it can be fun to look at things differently.

Write a story from the monster's perspective. Here are a few "monstrous" ideas:

> Create a Monster.
>
> If you had to be a monster, what kind of monster would you be? Would you be big and hairy with four eyes and long fangs? Would you be a scaly dragon breathing fire? Would you be a multi-tentacled sea creature? When making your monster, also consider how the monster got that way. Genetic mutation caused by radiation? Witch's curse? Biogenetic engineering? Arrival from another planet?
>
> Misunderstood Monster.
>
> One of the most poignant scenes in horror cinema is from one of the original Frankenstein movies. The creature comes upon a girl by a pond picking flowers. He is attracted by the flowers, and wants to play with the girl. Someone sees him, and they scream, then the girl screams. Unaware of his own strength he accidentally kills the girl. Write a scene where your monster is misunderstood in some way.

4   CREATIVE CALISTHENICS

The Monster Under the Bed.

I'm not sure if, as children, we were scared of the monster under the bed or comforted by it. In a strange way, that monster was our own bedtime companion. It was, also, a good way to get Mom and Dad's attention. Imagine there really is a monster under your bed. What's life like for it? Does it get bored? Why is it under the bed and not out terrorizing the village?

Creating a scary monster, that's easy. Creating a sympathetic monster is much harder and much more fun.

MAGIC DOORS AND SECRET PASSAGES

Here are a couple of simple exercises to get your creative juices flowing:

The Magic Door.

You wake up. You go into any room of the house and notice a door that wasn't there the night before. Open it and describe what lies behind it.

The Sliding Bookcase.

You are cleaning the bookcase in your new house, or you are visiting a friend, and you tug on a book. The bookcase moves out of the way to reveal a secret passage. Where does that passage lead? What happens when you get to the end of it?

TELL ME A STORY   5

THE TRUNK IN THE ATTIC

I don't have an attic, but I do have a cedar chest I inherited from my mother. After she passed away, I went through the memories stored there. I found some tiny booties, a wedding dress, clippings of stories I wrote for the school newspaper, letters from my dad when he was stationed with the occupation forces in Japan after WWII, pictures of my grandparents, scrapbooks, baby clothes. Here lay 83 years of life stacked in a four-foot long wooden box.

We pack away our memories and let years go by without even looking at them, but those bits and pieces of life trapped in the things we cannot throw away tell a story. They tell many stories.

Here's an exercise. Your mother (or grandmother, aunt, best friend or those of a character in your story) has passed away. You are cleaning out the attic. You come across a trunk. You open the trunk. What do you find? Write about it. What story does it tell? How might what you find in it change your life? What secrets does it reveal?

For variety, it can be a garage or a storage closet or a maybe a four-foot long cedar chest.

PARABLES FOR A NEW MILLENNIUM

Wherever Jesus went, he taught the people using parables. A parable is simply a story. It is a story drawn from the people's daily experiences. Jesus used stories about weddings, planting a crop, fishing, searching for lost sheep, and other things common to his culture.

We no longer live in an agrarian society. So, it's time for some new parables. Write a parable for the modern-day person. Here are some starters:

The Kingdom of God is like unto a computer . . .

The Kingdom of God is like unto a GPS guidance system . . .

The Kingdom of God is like unto a PDA . . .

6   CREATIVE CALISTHENICS

The Kingdom of God is like unto a flat tire . . .

The Kingdom of God is like unto a sale at Macy's . . .

The Kingdom of God is like unto an e-mail . . .

I think that's enough to get you started.

ONLY ONE DAY

Ray Bradbury wrote a short story called "Last Night of the World." The premise was that everyone woke up one morning and "just knew" it was the last day of the world. Many creative works feature someone with a limited time to live. Two books that come to mind are *A Lesson before Dying* and *Tuesday's with Morrie*. There was also a 60s TV show starring Ben Gazzara called *Run for your Life* about a man with only a year to live. (Strangely enough, he survived on TV for three years. The miracles of media medicine.)

Why not give your character the bad news?

The doctor tells your main character that s/he will be dead by midnight. The person will be in good health until then. What does that character do with the time left? Describe their day.

Here's a more disturbing variation, but, if you have the courage to do it, you will benefit. You have only 24 hours to live. What do you do with the time?

Write a short story describing your day. Be honest. Don't write what you hope you would do. Write what you think you really would do.

Since most of our characters, stories, articles, essays and books come from within, understanding what's inside there helps make us better writers.

TIME MACHINE

Here is a fun exercise.

You sit down at the controls of a time machine. The dials spin randomly and land on a date. You open the door. What do you see?

You can randomize this exercise by writing some dates on pieces of paper and drawing one out by random. Write 1000 words describing what you see.

It's a good exercise for historical or science fiction writers.

KEEPSAKES

The original title for this was "Christmas Ornament Stories." Then I realized that Christmas had passed when I wrote it. However, the idea works for any type of keepsake.

Many of us have keepsakes around the house. Christmas ornaments are a perfect example. When I look at my tree, I see the plain blue and green globes that I bought for my first Christmas after I moved out on my own. Fewer remain, and they aren't very fancy, but they have a story behind them.

Then there are the ornaments given to me by my students over the years. A few I bought because a niece or a nephew wanted me to buy them. They were in charge of decorating the tree for several years.

I also collect Teddy Bears and tea pots. My mom has her collection of salt and pepper shakers collected from the places we visited when I was young. I can point to each and tell you where and when and why we bought them.

So, if you are stuck for an idea to get started writing, try pointing your attention at one of your keepsakes and begin writing about where that came from. You'll find the creativity of remembrance flooding through your heart and onto the page.

MUSICAL EXERCISES

I have to give credit to the Christian Fiction Writing Critique Group for the inspiration for this one. They were talking about a scenario where your work-in-progress was turned into a movie. The question was, "What songs would you like in the sound track?"

That reminded me of several musical exercises.

Let's start with the one I just mentioned. I would switch it around a bit and say, "What songs would be most appropriate for your story?" This could be because of the meaning of those songs or because the setting would be enhanced with that music playing in the background.

A second exercise has to do with characterization. When creating your character dossiers, include a section on favorite music. Here are a few ideas to show that in your writing:

What radio stations does s/he have preset on the car radio?

What CD is in the CD player right now?

If the character goes out to a concert on a date, who would be playing? Would his or her date enjoy the music?

What does the character sing in the shower?

Just as music can enhance a character, it can help set the scene. Background sounds can include music. Riding in an elevator, your character can be humming along with the elevator music. Loud rock and roll can be coming out of the Jukebox in some '60s drive-in. You could play against the stereotypes. We all have had the experience of some low-rider convertible blaring out hip-hop music at a street corner. What if they were playing Beethoven's 1812 Overture, complete with cannon blasts, instead?

Another thought is to have your characters interact with the background music. I had a man approach me once (when I was much younger and better looking) in a grocery store with the line, "If the Muzak were playing, I'd ask you to dance." I'm still looking for a place to use that in my stories. I can just see a couple dancing down the aisles of a grocery store as the Muzak plays.

These are just a few ways to make your writing sing.

WHAT IF . . .

This is an oldie, but a goodie. It involves looking at a situation and posing several possible scenarios. For instance, if you are a fiction writer, and you see a couple in a restaurant eating in absolute silence, start asking, yourself "What if?"

What if the phone rang, and they hear their son was killed in a traffic accident? What if the man threw water in his wife's face? What if the woman announced to the man that she is having an affair? What if . . . Well, you get the idea.

This is a classic for fiction writers, but it can work for nonfiction writers as well. Let's go back to that restaurant. The cash register rejects someone's credit card. You could ask, "What if a person's identity is stolen? How they can repair the damage?" You might see someone give the clerk a coupon and you could ask, "What if there was a way to produce coupons online? Would they work better, worse or the same as those in newspapers?"

Of course, this works best if you take a notepad with you to record your ideas. So, the next time you are out and about, don't forget to ask, "What if?"

WHAT HAPPENS NEXT

Here's one that I like personally.

Take a Bible story and write about what might have happened later. For instance, have you ever thought about what faced the lame beggar at the Gate Beautiful? For 38 years he has one identity—lame beggar. Now, he can walk, but what is he going to do with that? What type of job can he get? How does this change his relationships with family and friends? Every miracle has consequences. The question of what you do with a miracle is an interesting one. Speculation about this lead me to write a devotion about the consequences of the miraculous.

One I use in teaching involves what might have happened to the three Hebrew children after the fiery furnace. Can you imagine them six or eight months down the road? They are working in the palace and Shadrach says, "I don't know what I'm going to do. The provinces in the south want more gold for their grain. The king says not to give it to them. But if we don't we'll have a fam-" And Meshach says, "Hey, Shad, remember the fire?"

You get the idea. You can do the same thing with movies, books or short stories.

JUMPER CABLES
FOR
THE BRAIN

Sometimes, you feel like you are drained of all creative energy like a dead battery. When that happens, you need to jump start your imagination. This chapter has several exercises intended to do just that.

ARTIFACTS

One of my interests is ancient history. The History Channel is in *My Favorites* on the remote. For the most part, we know about what happened in the past by inferring a culture from their artifacts. For these exercises, you will be creating your own artifacts.

Digging Atlantis.

I love to scour thrift shops for odd items that look like they belong in another place and time. I have old vases, chains, broken pottery, even a necklace made out of little wooden pieces.

Some things I don't even have a clue as to their use. When I need a quick idea starter, I pull a couple of items out of this bag and imagine the following scenario:

The lost continent of Atlantis has arisen from the ocean, and these artifacts emerged from the excavation. What could I deduce about the civilization of that land based on these artifacts? What were the people like? How did the Atlanteans use these objects? What meaning did they have for the people? I might even write a short story about someone using the item.

Future Archeology.

In this variation, I pick an object in the room at random. I imagine that I'm an archeologist in the future, and the only thing that survived from the early 21st century is this object.

How might that future archeologist interpret our society from that object? What might s/he get right? Wrong? Partially right? I then write a short lecture the archeologist might give about the object.

These are both fun activities which are adaptable for writing classes or individual writing warm ups.

BALL, RULER AND HANGER

The first creativity exercise I can remember comes from a high school psychology class. Our teacher give this assignment: "Write down as many ways as possible to use a hollow rubber ball, a ruler and a hanger other than for their intended use. They can be used alone or in combination with the other objects." I think I came up with almost 50 ways.

This exercise is good for helping you look at the ordinary in extraordinary ways. Sometimes an idea for a crafts article spring from using an ordinary object in an unconventional way. In fiction, your character may be faced with a seemingly impossible situation and, with MacGyver-like genius, make use of some simple object to get out of trouble. Even devotions can be found in the ordinary objects of daily life if you look at the object, not for what it can do, but for what it can teach.

MORE THAN ONE ANSWER

A science teacher had this question on a test: "How would you use a barometer to find the height of a building?"

The correct answer involved calculation of air pressure at the base of the building compared to that on the roof. One student gave that answer along with nearly 20 others. Some of these included classics such as:

•Tie a string on the barometer, lower it from the top of the building and measure the string.

•Roll the barometer up the side of the building and count the number of revolutions and multiply by the circumference of the barometer.

•Drop the barometer from the top of the building and measure how long it takes to fall to the ground.

•Smash the barometer at the base of the building and count how many seconds it takes for the sound to reach the top of the building.

•Mark off degrees on the edge of the barometer, attach a straw to the center of the barometer and sight the top of the building. Use basic trigonometry to figure out the height of the building.

My personal favorite is, "Find someone who knows the height and say, 'I'll give you this neat barometer if you tell me the height of the building.'"

Sometimes, when faced with a writing problem, we think there is only one solution, but like our creative science student, we may find several solutions.

14   CREATIVE CALISTHENICS

For instance, you are having trouble coming up with the lead for a magazine article about keeping children safe when online. Instead of trying to come up with the one perfect introduction, write five in five different styles. Write one that begins with a story, one that begins with a quote, one that begins with a question, one that begins with a statistic and one that begins by setting the scene.

If you have written a story where your hero is faced with a moral choice, make a list of all the actions s/he might take including the ridiculous ones. Choose the one that advances the plot of the story while being true to the personality of the character.

The creative thinker rarely settles for just one answer.

A FUNNY THING HAPPENED ON THE WAY TO . . .

Have you ever thought about detours? You start going somewhere. Then right in the middle of the road is a detour. You have to go an entirely different way. Sometimes those detours are more interesting than the main road once you get over the irritation of having to go a different way.

Let's use a detour to get you on the road to a creative idea. Choose a couple of characters at random. Put them in a car going somewhere. Then right in the middle of the road appears a detour sign. Where does the detour take them? How do they react to the detour? What do they find down that road? How does the detour change everything?

Detours can be annoying and interesting. They can also be a great way to get a story started.

FREEWRITING

Back in the early 80s, I enrolled in a graduate program in the teaching of writing. Unfortunately, I discovered that most of the teachers who are teaching teachers how to teach writing couldn't write their way out of wet paper bag with a sharp pencil.

JUMPER CABLES FOR THE BRAIN   15

However, during that time, I was introduced to a book by Peter Elbow called *Writing without Teachers*. In this book, he introduced the concept of freewriting. Free writing is a technique to do two things. First, it helps you get started writing. Secondly, it is an intuitive technique for organizing your thoughts. I find it to be particularly useful if I'm having trouble getting started writing. Here's how it works.

You can use free writing with either fiction or nonfiction. I'll describe its use with nonfiction, but the basic procedures are the same for fiction.

First, I sit down and review my research. I leaf through all of my cards. I just browse. I'm not doing anything more than getting familiar with what I have read or heard in my interviews. Next, I put away my research and take about a 20 minute break.

At the end of this break, I begin to freewrite for 20 minutes. I set a timer and stop writing when the timer goes off.

What do I mean by freewriting?

What I mean is I simply sit down and write down what ever comes into my mind, and I keep writing for the full 20 minutes. I don't stop. I don't worry if it's related to the topic or not. Sometimes I've sat at my keyboard and typed things like "This topic is so boring. Why did I choose it? Why am I doing this stupid exercise? Isn't this an interesting color for a computer screen? I really need to clean my screen. I'm getting paid in two weeks. . . ."

Usually, after a few minutes of writing gibberish, I'll start writing about the topic. I don't necessarily write complete sentences. I simply write down whatever is coming to mind in whatever order it comes. When the timer goes off, I stop writing. I save that file and close the computer window. Then, I take another 20-minute break.

These breaks are important because they let my subconscious mind work on the project. I come back to the keyboard and write for another 20 minutes. I take another 20-minute break and return for another 20-minute free writing session.

By this time, my writing becomes a bit more coherent, and my thoughts more orderly. I put that third draft away overnight. The next day I take out my research, and I begin to use that third draft as the basis for writing my article.

In addition to being a good way to deal with writer's block, it also helps me get ready to write. It's like a stretching exercise before workout routine.

16   CREATIVE CALISTHENICS

Incidentally, Peter Elbow's book is still available. I recommended it for both beginning and experienced writers. I especially recommend it for anyone who is interested in teaching writing. It sets forth a student-centered approach, which is powerful.

GRAB BAG

When you can't seem to get going on a project, the most important thing to do is to write. That means write anything. It doesn't matter what you write. The quality doesn't matter. Just start writing.

This exercise helps get you writing and learning to think more creatively at the same time.

Keep a bag of odd items sitting somewhere in your office. They can be some if your kids broken toys, old kitchen gadgets, tools, old shoes, pine cones, and any other odds and ends you have laying around the house.

When you just can't get started writing, close your eyes, and stick your hand in the bag. Pull out the first thing it lands on. Don't search around for the thing you want. Just grab an item at random.

Set the object on the desk in front of your computer. Now, do one of two things with this item.

First, begin to describe the object in detail. Write down its size, color, shape and your impressions of it. Come up with some metaphors to describe it. What does it remind you of? Does it bring back memories? Write down those memories. In other words, write down anything you can think of in connection with this object.

The second exercise is one in basic creativity. Look at your object, and write down at least 30 ways to use the object other than for its intended use. For instance, if you grab a potholder, don't write down "to pick up a hot pot." Write down other uses for the potholder. For instance, "frame it as a work of art." Okay, it's a silly example. However, with creativity exercises, sometimes the silliest ideas are the best ones. Maybe an article for a crafts magazine: Framed potholders for birthday gifts.

JUMPER CABLES FOR THE BRAIN   17

INTERVIEW OF A LIFETIME

Have you ever wished that you could have interviewed the apostle Paul or King David or possibly Martin Luther? Why not do it?

Choose a character from the Bible (or history). Write out a list of a few questions for that character. Then put yourself into the shoes of that character, and answer the questions in the style of that character. You can use this both as a writing exercise and as a Bible study exercise.

A variation of this activity is to choose a character from one of your stories and interview that character. This can help give you some insight into your characters.

Another variation is to work on this with a partner. One of you prepares the questions, and the other writes the answers in character.

ONLY $39.95 PLUS SHIPPING AND HANDLING

Here's one my students enjoy. Create a product and write a script for an infomercial. What will this product do? Who would want it? What are the benefits of using the product? Why is this a bargain?

Try to do it in true infomercial style with over-the-top exclamations about how valuable these things are, how great a value you are getting, the fake breathless "limited-time" approach, how the product is going to change your life, that sort of thing.

Aside from being fun, this can help you think about things from a reader's perspective. These infomercial writers are masters of understanding what motivates a person. Taking a stroll in their shoes will teach you something about motivation.

PICTURE IT!

I keep a collection of provocative pictures in a file. Most are pictures that allow for some sort of interpretation. For instance, I have several of people looking out of the frame of the picture. Others are eyeball bender types of pictures.

I pick a picture at random. Then I write about what happened leading up to this picture, what followed it, or what the person sees outside the frame of the picture.

Why not start your picture collection. Then when you want to get writing pull out a picture and tell the story behind it.

WRITE AT FIRST SIGHT

As a warm up for your writing session, stand in the middle of the room, close your eyes and spin around. Open your eyes. Take the first thing that you see and write 500 words about it. You can describe it, write down your feelings about it, list a bunch of ways to use it, tell a story about it, or write an ad for it. It doesn't matter what you write, just write.

GETTING
IDEAS

"Where do you get your ideas?"

It's a question most professional writers get all too often. Frequently, we answer glibly that the problem is not getting ideas, but sorting through the mass of ideas we have for the few "gems" which will make for good stories. While true in the broadest possible terms, it doesn't tell the whole story. Sometimes, both beginner and pro start to scrape the bottom of the idea barrel. This chapter includes ways to refill that barrel to overflowing.

TOPIC SPOKING

Many of us come up with one-word topics for our articles. I get a lot of magazine writing students who give me topics like abortion, shyness, cancer, marriage, ecology, etc. The problem with these topics is that they are way too large. People write books on these topics. Additionally, they are not focused enough to target a given type of magazine.

Nevertheless, I like big topics. Why? Because they open the possibility of multiple original sales from a single body of research. However, that means I have to find the subtopics under the main topic. To do this I use a graphic approach called topic spoking.

How it works is that I draw a circle in the middle of a sheet of paper, and then draw lines out from it. I write my one-word topic in the circle. Next, I begin to brainstorm other markets and related subtopics on the "spokes." Under those spokes, I draw other lines as I further refine the topic. For instance, right now, I am beginning to research computer-mediated communication (CMC) for both trade and academic markets. So, my "spokes" are "family and CMC," "online education," "easy intimacy," "business," and "scholarly." Under "family and CMC" I have further narrowed it to "cyber-bullies," "cyber-adultery," "teaching kids about communicating on line," "cyber-etiquette: teaching kids about online courtesy."

You get the idea.

Incidentally, I've been using Office 2007. Word has a feature called "Smart Art." I use it to create a satellite design and adapt it to topic spoking. I may eventually abandon pencil and paper. Okay, maybe not, but it is a fun option.

FORMULA TITLES

If you read magazines regularly, you will notice that many article titles are built around set formulas. Sometimes, only one word will remove an article from *Christianity Today* and put it in *Today's Christian Woman*. These are not only formula titles, but also formula ideas. This is a quick way to get article ideas. Don't worry so much about whether these are good ideas or not. Just fill in the blanks.

1. _____Ways to Save Money on _____

2. _____Ways to _____ Better

3. How to _____

4. How a Church Improved its _____

GETTING IDEAS   21

5. How to Improve Your _____

6. How to Make _____

7. My Most _____ Experience

8. How to Raise Money _____ing.

9. The Most _____ Person I ever Met

10. _____: An Unforgettable Travel Experience

11. _____ Ways to Save Time _____ing.

12. Everything You Need to Know to _____

13. _____: An Unusual Person with an Unusual (Ministry/ Hobby/ Occupation/ Home)

14. The _____est _____ in _____

15. My Life as a _____

16. Easy to Make _____s

17. Your Ministry in _____

18. Have You Considered _____

19. _____ Made Easy

20. _____ Steps to _____

21. How to _____ on Your Own

22. Why You Should _____

23. Why _____ is _____

24. A New Way to _____

25. _____ and What You can do About it?

26. _____: A National Problem

27. _____: A Spiritual Problem

28. _____: An Opportunity for Profit

29. _____: What it Means to You

30. Who is _____

22   CREATIVE CALISTHENICS

31. How to _____ Naturally/ Inexpensively/ More efficiently

32. Improve Your Health by _____

33. Protect Yourself from _____

34. What one Church/Community did to _____

35. The Inspiring True Story of _____

IN THE PAPERS

Several years ago, I lived in Eugene Oregon, home of the University of Oregon. Go Ducks! I was reading the *Eugene Register-Guard* one day, and I saw a feature story about Susan Glaser, PhD. She was a shyness counselor at the university. She sounded intriguing. I called her and set up an interview. Out of that one interview, and a lot of library research, I sold five articles adding up to a total of about $1500 dollars.

Your local newspaper is a treasure trove of ideas for both nonfiction and fiction. Here are a few creative ways to use the newspaper to generate ideas.

Feature Stories.

Check out the lifestyles, business and sports sections for profiles of interesting local personalities and organizations. For instance, a story about a local hardware store owner who donates fire alarms to poor families could be a story for either a hardware trade journal or a firefighting magazine. If you find out the owner attends a certain church, write a third article for the church denominational publication.

News stories.

These are great sources of idea starters for fiction. I read a story about a fellow who robbed a bank. Police arrested him at the deli next door. He stopped to get a sandwich. What kind of person does that? Someone wanting to get caught? Why would

GETTING IDEAS   23

he want to get caught? What is the backstory to this guy? Could it be a fiction story. You have a six-car pile up on the freeway. How did everyone get there? Write their stories?

On the nonfiction side, a major drug bust could start you thinking about tips for parents to keep their kids off drugs. A story about record-breaking temperatures and drought conditions in your area, might lead to an article about the day-to-day impact of climate change on local communities. A story about a disabled soldier returning from Iraq might lead to a story about how churches are helping disabled soldiers. You get the idea.

Announcements.

Who is coming to town to perform or speak? This is your opportunity to get an interview. You say, but I'm not a "name" reporter. I won't get an interview. Well, you won't get that interview if you don't ask. I'm not a "name" reporter, but I've interviewed governors, senators, Christian "rock stars," evangelists and others simply because I asked.

Look at the listings of conventions and conferences coming to your community. Back in the 80s, when computers were just entering the classroom, I wangled an invitation to a conference on the subject. I had access to all the workshops and vendors. I also had access to most of the presenters. I got enough information for a half dozen articles.

So, the next time you read a newspaper, keep a pencil and pad handy. You could find your next story idea.

IN YOUR DREAMS

I like this one because it works while you are asleep. The idea is a simple one. Keep a pencil and pad on your bed stand. Upon awakening, jot down a few notes about your dreams. Don't worry if they don't make any sense. Dreams aren't supposed to make sense. However, the stories they tell, absurd as they may seem, often contain a germ of true inspiration dredged up from the depths of the subconscious. I've written two short stories that had their roots in dreams. Who knows what I will "dream up" tonight.

THINK OUTSIDE THE LYRICS: NONFICTION

Sometimes, when listening to music, you just have to think outside the lyrics. Seriously, let your mind go free, and you will be surprised what might come to mind. Some examples off the top of my head:

Moon River.

◆a popular science article about water on the moon. What that means for the future of lunar colonization?

◆building a reflecting pond in the backyard so you can watch the moon

Green, Green Grass of Home.

◆how to grow a lush lawn

◆marijuana use among Baby Boomer yuppies

◆greening your house. Ecologically sensitive ways to do everything around the house

I Left My Heart in San Francisco.

◆a Tony Bennett Tour of the City by the Bay highlighting the landmarks mentioned in the song.

GETTING IDEAS   25

◆an essay about music of cities and what they tell about the residents.
◆a profile of Tony Bennett at 80.

It's Only a Paper Moon.
◆making dioramas with your kids to teach them about the Bible.
◆an essay about the trend toward the artificial in the modern world.

Well, you get the idea. That was about 10 minutes of work. Now, you try it.

THINK OUTSIDE THE LYRICS: FICTION

I know that some authors have a "sound track" for their writing. Their sound track is a collection of songs that reflect the various themes of the novel. I'm going to suggest that songs can also stimulate your creativity in other ways. Songs can give you ideas for writing.

Let's take a song like Scarborough Fair. The refrain goes:

Are you going to Scarborough Fair?
Parsley, Sage, Rosemary and Thyme
Remember me to one who lives there
She once was a true love of mine

There are many possibilities with a ballad like this. One is to imagine the 'backstory' of the song. Who is the singer? Who did he know? Who was his true love. How did that love affair go? How did it end? Why did he leave? Why does he still remember her? Write a story about that experience which leads up to the song. You could also write one about what happens after the song. What happens when this person goes and "remembers" the singer to his former love? Does she return to the singer? Does she fall in love with the messenger? Lots of ways to go.

So, listen to songs, not only as a background for your writing, but stay tuned to them, and they may become your inspiration as well.

YOU CAN QUOTE ME ON THAT

When I was in junior high, I discovered a wonderful book. It was called *Bartlett's Familiar Quotations*. You name the subject, there were a bunch of quotes related to the subject. It certainly is a good reference volume, and it is a great way to spice up your nonfiction writing with a pithy quote at just the right place, but it can also be an idea machine.

You don't have to go to the library anymore to search this and other collections of quotes. There is a website at http://www.bartleby.com/100/ where you can plug in a word and get a bunch of quotes on that subject. Here's a quote I found on the subject of family:

> Family lore can be a bore, but only when you are hearing it, never when you are relating it to the ones who will be carrying it on for you. A family without a storyteller or two has no way to make sense out of their past and no way to get a sense of themselves.

Looking at that quote, I can think of a number of writing ideas like:

+how to put together a family history

+family story nights when the family gets together to tell stories and eat popcorn

+an article about the art of storytelling

+a fiction piece about a world where the most important person is the family storyteller

+a reminiscence piece about the stories your parents told, and how precious the memories of those stories are now that they are gone.

So, if you are looking for some good writing ideas, why not talk to my old friend John Bartlett.

POSSESSION OF THE GOOD: NONFICTION

One of the first things I learned in college, which I didn't already know from high school (our high school was pretty good so the first two years of college were mostly an advanced review), was a quote from Aristotle's Rhetoric. Aristotle wrote, "There is an object at which all men aim in any action which they choose or avoid; and that object may be called happiness or possession of The Good."

Aristotle coined a word for his concept of "The Good": *kaloskagathos*. It combines two Greek words kalos meaning good, useful, beautiful (that is a good painting) and agathos meaning moral goodness (Jesus was a Good Man). What he is saying is that people are motivated by the attempt to acquire that which they consider useful and/ or morally acceptable.

So, what does this have to do with writing? When it comes to nonfiction writing, it means that you need to determine what your audience values when coming up with ideas for articles.

For instance, I am assuming that readers of this book value anything that will help them learn to write and to publish what they write. Therefore, I am producing creativity tips, writing prompts and the like. If I put out tips on growing roses, some of you might be interested, but most of you would not. However, in a book entitled *Growing Prize Winning Roses* tips about writing probably wouldn't be so popular. Why? Because that is not the perception of "The Good" shared by the readers of that book.

So, let's put this into practice. Get a copy of a magazine or log on to a webzine where you would like to publish an article. Read each article. After reading the article, in one word to one sentence, write down what "The Good" was that the reader would gain from that article. Do the same with the ads.

What did the advertiser assume is The Good that motivates a person to purchase that product or service?

Look over your list of "Goods." Do you see a trend? Take three of these and brainstorm at least 10 article ideas that address that "Good" in some way.

A WORD FROM OUR SPONSOR

What do you do when the commercial comes on? Get a snack? Surf other channels? Attend to other - er - personal matters? Well, if you are a nonfiction writer, you may be missing a potential source of article ideas.

Every product you see advertised is designed to solve a problem. . That problem may be getting from point A to point B. It may be getting from point A to point B without emptying your bank account on gas. It may be feeding your family. It may be looking good to the neighbors. Within every product is an implied solution to a problem.

Products address problems. Your articles can address the same problems. So, sit down with a paper and pen. During your next commercial break, write down the products, the problem addressed and a magazine that might also address that problem.

For instance, I just saw a commercial about a "Power Juicer." The problem addressed in the commercial is that people don't eat as healthily as they should, and that a juicer will help them get a full compliment of fruits and vegetables every day. Immediately, *Prevention* magazine comes to mind, but also *Cuisine and Parents.*

Do this during an entire evening of TV watching. Look at your list of problems and magazines. Choose the problems addressed by the magazines you have targeted for publication.

Write down two article ideas for each of these problems. Write down each idea that comes to mind even if you think it is either stupid or something you couldn't write. Even the stupid ideas may stimulate your thinking.

A variation on this is to choose a magazine for which you want to write. Look at the ads in that magazine and do the same thing. Remember, advertisers are trying to help people solve the same problems that editors are. They often know more about the audience of a particular publication than even the editorial staff.

Therefore, the next time you run across an ad, don't consider it a nuisance. Consider it an opportunity.

GETTING IDEAS 29

WORK A BEAT

Back in the late 1970s, a student graduated from our journalism school. He moved to Marin County in California right in the middle of Silicon Valley. He had some technical background along with his journalism degree. He started dropping by the public relations offices of the various tech companies picking up press releases about the new technologies and chatting with engineers, scientists, and executives. He rewrote and enhanced the press releases and sold the articles to both trade journals and general interest tech magazines. In the late 1970s, he was making $50,000 a year doing this.

He carved out a niche for his writing, by working a beat. This journalistic term refers to being proactive about visiting news sources in a given field on a regular basis. Let's say you are a member of a particular denomination, once a month you can call or visit each church of that denomination in your area to see if they are doing anything that might be of interest to denominational magazines or local publications.

There's also a side benefit of this approach. Once you sell a few articles, these people will start calling you with tips, and sometimes they will hire you to do private jobs for them. I was doing this for a while with some bed and breakfast inns. I wrote several articles for travel and architecture magazines. Additionally, several inn operators hired me to write promotional materials for their inns.

Another advantage of that beat was, if I showed up for breakfast, I ate well.

TITLE SWITCH

We all know that magazine writers should write with a specific market in mind. You can take this to mean either a specific magazine or a specific type of magazine. This exercise is designed to generate a large number of targeted magazine article ideas.

Get a copy of a magazine representative of your target market. Make a list of the titles in that magazine. Now, change one or two words in each title to create a new topic.

30   CREATIVE CALISTHENICS

For instance, a Christian women's magazine might have the article, "Ten Things God Taught me through my Children." You could change that to "Ten Things God Taught me through my husband/ grandchildren/ boss/ parakeet."

Try to come up with at least two or three variations on each title. It is a great way to study a magazine's content and get ideas at the same time.

OUT
AND
ABOUT

Writing can be a pretty solitary task. You sit in your office pounding out words on a computer. Before you end up a literary hermit, find some ways to stimulate your writing by getting out from behind your desk with some of these exercises that get you "out and about."

IDEAS IN AN ART GALLERY

I'm a total academic. I love museums, libraries and art galleries. They inspire me. Sometimes, I get writing ideas while spending time in them.

Following are a few exercises you can do in an art gallery. Since most art galleries and museums have places to sit and look at the paintings, take your notepad along.

32   CREATIVE CALISTHENICS

1. Imagine you are one of your characters strolling through the gallery. Describe one of the pictures/sculptures in his or her words. Jot down a few notes about what they think about this artwork, and about what emotions that painting or sculpture engenders in them.

2. Go to the abstract art portion of the gallery. Without looking at the author's title for the piece, write one of your own. Jot down the emotions you feel while looking at this work. Write down what there is in that painting that causes you to feel that way. Is there a way you can use the same imagery, only in words, to evoke a similar emotion?

3. Place yourself in front of a realistic painting with some people in the picture. Jot down back stories for those characters, then what brought them to this scene, and what is going on outside the "window" of the frame.

4. Write a 50-100 word description of one of the paintings. Try to touch not only on what the painting looks like, but also how it feels.

AN EASY CHAIR AND SOME MAGAZINES

Today, many of us shun the library in favor of the internet, but if you want to write for magazines, you need to read magazines. I don't mean online versions of magazines either. The internet versions are usually shortened versions of the print publication. Even if they feature full-length articles, the experience is different. You need to have the experience of the reader. You need to see the ads. You need to feel the paper and smell the ink.

This is where the library easy chairs come into play. Go to your local library's periodicals room. Which ones represent the types of magazines for which you would like to write? Take them off the shelves and begin to browse through them. Make a list of the types of articles contained in each. Try to categorize them. Some good categories include how to, personal experience, profile, problem exposition, general informative, argumentative, inspirational, devotional, etc. How many do they have of each? Choose the top five categories. Brainstorm at least 10 ideas for each category. Don't worry about the quality of those ideas. This is about quantity not quality.

Another idea generator: Look at the ads. Make a list of the products. Write down ideas generated by those ads. For instance, if you see lots of auto ads, you might generate ideas such as ways to save money on gas, how to choose a safe car, how to negotiate a price on a car, how much car insurance do you need, etc.

So, turn off the computer and spend some time in the library.

CREATIVITY ON THE ROAD

We all need a break once in awhile. Sometimes, it is good to just get out of town and take a vacation. At the risk of encouraging workaholic behavior, I thought I'd present a few ways that you can keep your creative muscles limber while still enjoying your vacation:

Who Lives There?

This is a nice game to take the place of "Are we there yet?" It's a game which encourages imagination in both children and adults One person acts as the director of the game. That person chooses a house and someone in the car and says, "Blue house on the right. Johnny, who lives there?" Johnny, then, has to tell a story about the people who might live in that house.

Variations include: "Who's in that car/ airport? Where are they going?"

Travel Article Ideas.

Destination Pieces. Keep a notebook of interesting, but little known travel destinations. The major ones have been done to death, but, perhaps, you have found the perfect uncrowned getaway. Take a few pictures, pick up brochures and get a contact number. When you get home, call back for an interview with the owner. Remember, this is a vacation, don't take time away from your family to cover the story.

Survival on the road pieces. Maybe, while traveling, you found the perfect way to keep the kids amused or to eat healthy foods while on the road. Jot down the idea in your idea book, and then work on it later at home.

Picture prompts.

You are going to be taking a bunch of pictures anyway. Why not take pictures of interesting locations that you might use in your stories. Take provocative pictures like the 50-foot tall chef in front of a restaurant or the old man and his grandson sitting on a park bench in the theme park eating ice cream. When you get home and need something to get you writing, pull out one of the pictures and begin writing about it.

Devotional ideas.

I've gotten so many ideas for devotions while traveling. The road itself is a metaphor for life, and things like accidents, detours, signs, country roads and highways all teach us something about living.

I remember driving by a big, old, second hand shop. It stretched almost a block. At one end was a sign that read: "We buy Junk." At the other end was another sign reading: "We sell Antiques." I have written devotions and Bible studies using that example.

Another time, I saw a huge man walking with his three or four-year-old son. The boy was pulling this mountain of a man around everywhere. The guy looked so tired, but at the same time the child looked so happy, and you could tell that also made the father happy.

I thought about God and us. We think we are pulling God around, but, really, he just lets us have our way up to a point. I knew if the boy started to run into the street, the mountain would pull back.

Newspapers.

I always pick up a newspaper in every town I visit. It's amazing the writing ideas you can find on the feature pages or the business section. I imagine they might even be found on the sports page, but that's not my area of interest.

Maybe a local business won a national award, or the local high school has an unusual program for teaching art to inner city kids. Maybe a church celebrates its 100th anniversary as the first church of that denomination in the state. Sometimes a gem of a good magazine article can be found in the pages of a local newspaper.

MALL WATCHING

Let's go to the mall. Consider it a perfect excuse to browse to your heart's content, and, if anyone asks, you can say you are a writer researching a story.

Fiction.

Look around the store and at the people in the store. Look at both shoppers and employees. Think about what brought those shoppers into the store. There's a story behind each product bought. Imagine that story. Now, look at the employees. Why are they there? This probably isn't their life's career. What do they want? How do they relate to each other? Watch the interaction between them and the shoppers. Sit down outside and jot down your impressions of these characters. Build some back stories for them.

Another good fiction idea is a little game I call "What's in that package?" Position yourself somewhere where you can watch people coming and going from the shops. Look at the packages and guess what's in the package. What did they buy? Why did they buy it? In your mind, follow them home. (Only do this in your mind. If you do so in person, you might get arrested.) Think about what they are going to do with that object. Is it a teenage girl's prom dress? Is it a pair of pajamas for a bed ridden, terminal parent? Is it paint for a new nursery? A wedding ring? Books for school?

Each purchase has a back story, use your imagination to figure it out.

Nonfiction.

Look at the products on sale. How are they displayed? What do these products tell us about trends in society? What are their functions? Are you good at using one of them? Could you write an article/handbook on how to use it? Can you think of unusual uses for ordinary items? What about some of the items that is interesting, weird or bizarre? Is there a story behind that item?

Brainstorm at least 10 ideas from each store and visit at least five stores. Remember, with brainstorming, you write down every idea even the stupid ones.

36   CREATIVE CALISTHENICS

If you break away from the mall and go to an area featuring locally-owned and operated businesses, look for interesting businesses, displays and promotional ideas. Trade journals love those kind of stories.

Back in the early 1980s, I saw a take-and-bake pizza place in our town. There were hardly any such places around back then. I arranged to interview the owner and got a great story for an entrepreneurial magazine. The article took an hour for the interview and maybe two hours to write. The magazine paid me $100 for it.

What's Down that Road?

I have to credit my Dad for this one. I used to live in Eugene, Oregon, and my folks lived in Eureka, California. Because of this, we traveled I-5 through southern Oregon almost once a month. As we drove along, we saw signs indicating small towns with names like Wolf Creek and Merlin. My Dad always said "One day, I'm going to just drive down into those little towns and look around." We never did. However, that doesn't mean I can't do that in my imagination.

Pull out a map and find towns with interesting names. Without going there, write a description of Main Street based on the name. Then describe the people who live there. What is the main industry? What type of people are they? How would they react to outsiders? For instance, in our area we have a town named Raisin City. You can guess what that town looks like. I see it filled with farmers and farm workers, a main street lined with mom and pop businesses, a convenience store, an old gas station with a garage and a 50s vintage tow truck. The feed and seed store on the corner has a bench out in front where the old men gather to remember old times. A thin patina of dust coats everything.

Of course, I may visit there someday and find a McDonald's and a string of trendy boutiques. It doesn't matter; it's all about using the imagination.

My dad's in heaven now. I wonder if, from there, he has a chance to see what life is like in those little towns.

OUT AND ABOUT   37

HOW'D THEY GET HERE?

This weekend I went to San Francisco. Instead of battling the traffic on the Bay Bridge, I parked at a station and took BART into the city. (For those not on the West Coast, BART stands for Bay Area Rapid Transit; a regional train and subway system that links most of the cities in the Bay Area.)

Riding the train reminded me of a little game I used to play called "How'd they get here." I pick out someone on the train. I look at the person. I create a little story in my head about why they are riding this train on this day to that city. I look for clues like how they are dressed, if they have someone with them, and what they are carrying. I create a scenario in my mind about the events that led up to them being on the train.

You can do this in your head or in a notebook. You can do it on the train or when you get home. If nothing else, it's a great way to pass the time.

THE BULLETIN BOARD BEAT

I worked for two years on the newspaper at one college. The next year, I transferred to another school. When I got there, I found myself the new kid on the block competing against seniors and grad students for the "plum" reporting assignments. So, what was I assigned? They gave me the library beat and the bulletin board beat. Eventually, I worked the library beat into a regular column, but some of my best stories came from the bulletin boards.

Bulletin boards are treasure troves of ideas for articles, short stories, interviews and local reviews. For instance, suppose you see a poster for a self-help seminar on retirement planning for 30 year olds. You could interview the presenter for a parenting magazine article called "IRAs and Orthodontists: Saving for retirement while the kids are home." A flyer about a concert with a prominent Christian artist might be an interview possibility. A lost kitten announcement could be the start of a children's story.

So, get up and out from behind the computer and check out the bulletin boards at the laundromat, the library, the bookstore and the college campus, but don't be surprised if you see a low-status school reporter combing through the notices with you.

38 CREATIVE CALISTHENICS

GOING ON VACATION

I'm getting ready to go on vacation, and I'm thinking travel. I'm going to the Bay Area (San Francisco Bay, that is) until next Wednesday. It will be fun and, hopefully, restorative. However, it got me thinking about vacations, and here are a few vacation-oriented writing starters:

1. Send your characters on vacation. Write a scene (whether it will go into your story or not) in which your characters go on vacation. You can make it a terrible vacation or put them all in a tight place like a cabin with two bedrooms and 6 adults. It's a good way to get to know your characters.

2. Choose a dream spot for a vacation. Research it and then write an imaginative diary about your trip there. A variation on this is to write your diary of a "fantastic" vacation to some place like the Moon, some historical period in the past or future, an alternate universe (like Narnia or Middle Earth) or a fantasy world of your own making.

3. While on vacation, make notes of places you visit and take plenty of pictures. Write "destination" pieces for travel magazines. You might also leave your card with places like tourist attractions and bed and breakfast inns. You would be surprised how many of these places want to be included in guidebooks, but they need someone to write a blurb for them.

STROLL AROUND TOWN

Every writer needs a lot of good writing ideas and a good library of sample magazines. This is a way to get both.

Go down to the business district in your town or a shopping center. The best place to work is a place with plenty of locally-owned businesses. Walk into the business and ask to speak to the owner or manager. Then say something like this: "Hi, I'm a writer, and I am considering writing some articles

OUT AND ABOUT   39

about businesses like yours. Do you have any back copies of any trade journals in your field I could have or borrow." As the person is giving you the
magazines, you can ask, "What types of things would you like to see in these
magazines which would help you in your business?"

Another good question is, "What have you learned about this business
you think I should know before writing for one of these publications?" A
question that can lead to a story is "What promotions have you run which
you have found particularly successful?"

A variation on this is to visit churches and ask for denominational magazines. You can also ask what types of interesting programs the church has
run which have been successful.

After this initial introduction and reading the magazines, if you find a
particular businessn field or group of churches interests you, make a list of
them and contact them on a regular basis.

Other variations include visiting the public information offices of schools,
colleges and universities or corporate offices of various businesses.

Back in journalism school, we called it working a beat. I'm older now and
bit more laid back. Today, I call it strolling around town.

BIOGRAPHIES FOR EVERYONE

I wish I could take credit for this one, but I can't. I knew a wonderful old
gentleman, a retired college professor, who did this. This may become more
than an exercise. It is a way to get some practice writing, but also to minister
to others.

He observed that most of us only make it into the newspaper three times
in our lives: when we are born, when we get married and when we die. What
he did was visit nursing homes and interview the residents about their lives.
He then took these interviews and wrote mini-biographies of the residents.
He collected them into small booklets that he distributed at the nursing
home. Just to put this into perspective, he did this before the advent of the
personal computer. With modern word-processing and desktop publishing
software, this is an even easier task.

This is a wonderful ministry, but it's also a good exercise. Nonfiction writers need to develop strong interview skills. Individuals who have a great deal of life experience and who are living in nursing homes are great interview subjects. They're willing to speak to you at length about their lives, their experiences, and the wisdom that they have gained through their lives.

Who knows, you might also discover a wealth of article and story ideas as well.

CHARACTERS AND SETTINGS

Stories are about people in places doing things. For your stories to come alive for your reader, you need to have memorable characters and vivid settings. In this chapter, you'll find a variety of exercises designed to help you develop characters and settings your readers will love.

BACKGROUND CHECK

If you find yourself wondering what your character might do next, then you may need to get to know your character better. Try this exercise. Pretend that your character is under a police investigation as a *person of interest*. The detective turns to his sidekick and says, "Run a background check on ___" What would they find?

CREATIVE CALISTHENICS

What's their credit like?

What are some of their past jobs?

What's their education?

Were they ever arrested? For what?

Where did they live before the start of the story?

Do they have relatives? Who are they? Where do they live?

What organizations do they belong to?

How many times have they been married?

Do they have children? Grandchildren?

What are their hobbies?

What awards have they won?

Where do they work?

Where did they work in the past?

Even if none of this goes into the story itself, it helps you understand that character. That understanding will make it easier to know how that character will respond when he or she gets into some sticky situation.

EULOGIES

My mother used to say, "Live your life so the preacher doesn't have to lie at your funeral." She had seen it on a reader board at a church somewhere. It's not bad advice for living, but I used it as a trigger for a writing exercise.

The exercise is simple. Imagine that one of the characters in your story dies unexpectedly, and another one of those characters has to give the eulogy. They only have three minutes. What would they say? Figuring that out will give you an insight into both characters. To spice it up a bit, imagine that the antagonist gives the eulogy for the protagonist or vice versa.

HOME BEAUTIFUL

Everybody has to live somewhere. Whether it is a mansion on Nob Hill or a cardboard box in the Tenderloin, it's home to somebody. Where does your character live? Here are three ideas for bringing your characters home to the readers:

Create a Floor Plan.

What direction does you character turn when leaving the kitchen for the living room? Is her bedroom at the rear of the house? Is his study so close to the kitchen he can smell the roast cooking in the oven? A simple way to keep track is to draw a floor plan of the house. You can base it on a real floor plan or create your own. If you want to get fancy about it, you can buy computer programs that will help you lay out your rooms complete with furniture.

Decorating style.

Describe your character's decorating style. Is it ultra-modern, colonial or country cozy. Maybe it's eclectic. Maybe it's just a jumble of stuff s/he likes. How does your character feel about the décor? Is the husband happy with his wife's choices for his study? Is the wife happy about her decision to let her husband decorate the den? How does the parent feel about the posters of pop stars adorning the walls of their teenage daughter's room?

Real Estate Brochure.

Pretend that your main characters are selling their home. Write up a brochure. Cut pictures out of magazines to illustrate the rooms. What are the big selling points for the home? Large backyard? Pool? Close to schools?

FIND THE EMOTION INSIDE YOU

You have probably heard of method acting where the actor finds in himself or herself the emotions the character is feeling and uses that to create a depiction of that character. Well, that's a good way to understand the emotions of your characters as well.

It starts with a sense memory of an event. Let's say your character is being chased by bad guys. S/he is running for his or her life. Take a piece of paper and write down a detailed description of some time when you were terribly scared of something. Be specific. What were your feelings? Did your heart pound? Did you perspire? What did the perspiration feel like? Smell like? Taste like? What about your breathing? Since your character is running, remember a time when you were running (whether you were running from someone or not). What was that like? Pain in the balls of the foot, blisters, limping, perspiration burning the eyes?

Once you have those memories clearly in mind, write the scene.

HELP WANTED: GREAT CHARACTERS

Many fiction writers are all about plot. We come up with a great premise and a bit of a plot. Then, we realize that plots and premises are fine, but it's people who make the story go forward. Even when we have a good idea of what the main characters might be like, we have the supporting cast and a whole host of "bit parts." To help get a good idea of what these characters are like write a help wanted announcement. Here's one for my work in progress which takes place in an underground settlement on the moon which looks a lot like a small town.

> Wanted: proprietor of a general store on the moon. Must be conversant with the odds and ends of daily life. From everyday china to hammers, nails, screwdrivers, screws and umbrellas. Your job is to keep people supplied with what they need. You should also be able to deliver a little folksy wisdom. If people underestimate you or consider you eccentric all the better. Some side work as a spy may be included in your duties.

CHARACTERS AND SETTINGS   45

A follow up to this exercise would be to write out a series of interview questions for different "applicants" for the job. What would they list as their qualifications, prior jobs, hobbies, skills, etc. It can be a different and enjoyable way to create a backstory.

AWARD DINNER

I came up with this one while talking to one of the other speech instructors at the college. One assignment she gives is: Prepare a presentation speech for an awards banquet. I thought, *What a great idea for developing a fiction character.*

One of your characters is receiving an award. What award is it? Who presents it to him/her? What does the presenter say about the recipient? How does your character feel about the award? What does he or she say when accepting the award?

ALL THE LITTLE PEOPLE

I have collected books since I was a child. I still have a bunch of Golden books my grandniece (who I believe to be grand in many ways) reads. One of the biggest parts of my personal library is the history section with about 300 books. I love history. No, not because of the wars and battles and dates and proclamations and stuff. I love history because of the people. I don't mean the "important" people. Sure, I am fascinated by the craziness of the Tsars, the cruelty of the later Caesars and the bravery of the explorers, but I am also interested in the ordinary lives of people in the past. If you love, history here is an interesting exercise:

A king cannot rule by fiat alone. He must have others help him. From people to keep track of the treasure room to someone to turn down the bed at night, "important" people usually have a cadre of lesser lights who brighten the path before they walk it.

46   CREATIVE CALISTHENICS

Write a diary in the character of one of these "little people." Some possibilities:

You are a maid in the Nixon White House during Watergate

You are a servant to King David

You are a shield bearer for a Pharaoh

You are a student of Socrates

You are an assistant to Thomas Edison

You are an assistant to Charles Finney

You were a communications officer during the Apollo 13 crisis

You can probably think of others. Choose a historical character that fascinates you and join their entourage.

WHAT'S ON THEIR BOOKSHELVES?

I recently went out of town for a few days. When I returned, my sister and brother-in-law surprised me by building an enormous book case. It stretches from ceiling to floor across half the wall. To a bibliophile, it is a beautiful thing to see so many books lining the wall of my living room.

It started me thinking. We definitely reveal ourselves by what we read. So, why not take a few moments now and write down a few book titles you might find on your main character's bookshelves. Also jot down the type of books s/he likes. If you were going to give your main character a book for Christmas, what would it be?

It's a wonderful thing when home decorating meets intellectual inquiry.

CHARACTERS AND SETTINGS   47

BAD CHOICES

Have you ever made a bad choice? I don't mean getting that horrid blouse with the big purple flowers on it. I mean something that affected your life in some significant way. We all have. God lets us mess up occasionally so that we can learn. What about your characters? Have they made any bad choices?

Take one of your main characters and write a scene in which a bad choice they made came back to haunt them. It doesn't mean you need to use it in the story, but it may help you get to know your character a bit better.

BUILD A CHARACTER

I believe that writer's groups should do more than just talk about writing or hear writers talk about writing. I like to engage them in actual writing or doing creative exercises. This one is great for either group or individual exercise.

Here's what you do. Get a bunch of file cards and a box with dividers. Create 10 dividers: Occupation, gender, age, nationality, height, weight, age, mood, general outlook on life, conversational style, and novel characteristics.

Create cards under each of these categories. Keep adding to them as other characteristics come to mind. To warm up to writing, pull cards at random out of the box. You might end up with a female prizefighter who is currently depressed. However, she usually has an optimistic outlook on life. She is indirect in her conversational style, and she writes poetry on the side.

Take about ten minutes and write a bit of her story. Where is she now? How did she get there? What is she be doing? Another idea is to interview this person on paper.

As a co-operative exercise, you and another person could both pull out cards; together you create a small scene with your characters and perform it for your writers group.

You probably won't use these precise characters in a story, but you might get some ideas for creating characters that are more complex.

48   CREATIVE CALISTHENICS

FAVORITES

When I go to my favorite restaurant, the waitress automatically gets me iced tea. She knows that I like honey mustard dressing on my salad, but I can't eat beans so she doesn't add the three-bean garnish. At home, I drink diet Dr. Pepper and lemon spice tea. Why am I telling you this? Because they are some of my favorite things, and they are part of what defines me.

Here's a little exercise. Take each of your main characters and make a "favorites" list. Include each of the following: food, color, drink, restaurant, car, TV show, books, types of reading material, movies, furniture/ decorating style, Bible translation, personality traits, clothing styles and anything else you think will help set your character apart from the other characters in your story.

It's amazing how small things become associated with specific characters. In the *Star Trek* franchise, a favorite drink defined many of the characters. Captain Picard liked Earl Grey Tea, Captain Janeway preferred coffee, Counselor Troi liked her hot cocoa, and the Klingon Warrior and security officer Lt. Worf was partial to prune juice.

These little lists of favorites won't compensate for a poorly thought out back story or lack of complexity in your characters, but they can add texture to them and make them real to your readers.

POSSESSION OF THE GOOD: FICTION

As you read the title to this exercise, you may be saying to yourself, "Hold on! Didn't we cover "Possession of the Good" in another chapter?"

Right you are, O perceptive one. However, in that exercise we were talking about generating nonfiction ideas. In this chapter we discover that this ancient concept can help us build great fictional characters as well.

Just to review, Aristotle said that every action we take is motivated by an attempt to "possess The Good." We saw that the term for "good" here is a combination of two Greek words. One meant good as in useful or beautiful and the other meant morally good.

CHARACTERS AND SETTINGS   49

So, you ask, how will this help build better characters? Your characters do things. The question you must ask before they do them is "Why?" We have all read bad literature where characters just do things to advance the plot without there being no clear motivation for them to do so.

One cliché from the movies is the shy, wimpy, scaredy-cat woman, who, upon hearing a noise in the room down the hall, instead of calling 911 and running out of the house, takes a flashlight and opens the door to the room to see what's going on.

We all say, "Give me a break!" We know it is out of character for her to do so. When we ask what this character with this personality expects to achieve by doing such a "courageous" act, we don't know.

Now, if it has been built into the script that she has called the police one too many times about imaginary threats, and she is trying to overcome her own paranoia, then it makes sense for her to do this possibly foolhardy thing. Her concept of The Good (overcoming her fears) outweighs the threat.

Go back to each of your characters and ask yourself, "What is this character's concept of The Good in this scene. What do they hope to accomplish? How will this act help them achieve that?" If you can't come up with a satisfying answer, then you need to revise either the character or the plot so that the action makes sense.

Many fictional villains, especially those in action-oriented fiction, seem to lack motivation. The classic is the one where the villain decides to do something that will destroy the world. Hello! You are on the world you are ready to destroy. Unless you write into this characters arc that he is suicidal, you have a real problem with motivation. At a less obvious level, why do the bullies in the youth novel harass the kid? What does the drunken husband expect to accomplish by drinking? What is the concept of The Good that drives the evil brother to the king in the fantasy novel to attempt a palace coup?

Ask yourself, "What do my characters want when they do things?" Write according to your answer.

50   CREATIVE CALISTHENICS

I'VE GOT A SECRET

Remember the old-time TV Game show "I've Got a Secret"? Okay, maybe not, if you are under 50. The show had guests who had a secret of some sort. A panel of celebrities asked "yes or no" questions trying to guess the secret, with a fair amount of wisecracking.

Most of us have secrets. Some are innocuous like the exact recipe for Grandma's chocolate chip cookies. Others may be practical matters like how much your business is ready to bid on a government project. Some we keep secrets out of fear of censure or ridicule like a misspent youth or having sold used cars. Some are darker like an addiction or hatred for another church member.

What secrets do your characters keep? From whom do they keep these secrets?

Why do they keep them? Try writing a scene in which your character either reveals his/ her secret voluntarily or has it revealed for him/ her. How does the character feel? Why did he/ she reveal it? How did the other characters react when they knew the secret? Was it how the main character expected them to react? If not, how did it differ?

Even nonfiction writers can use secrets to generate ideas.

Make a list of things people might keep secret such as bulimia, watching porn, marriage to an alcoholic, dyslexia, the identity of a birth parent in an adoption, attitudes, etc. List at least 10. Under each one, write down at least two article ideas.

For instance, addiction to internet pornography is a big problem and a secret many Christians keep. You might write an article about a group of men who hold each other accountable by installing monitoring software on each other's computers or a self-help article about how to talk to a spouse who's an addict.

It's not just a game show guest who can turn a secret into gold.

CHARACTERS AND SETTINGS 51

SEND YOUR CHARACTER BACK TO SCHOOL

A former boss of mine would call certain days "wild turkey" days. Well, I've had two "wild turkey" weeks. They are just now settling down. I've been writing original learning units for two classes and transforming them into online formats like programmed learning modules. Let's just say I spent about 50 hours one week doing this. It started me thinking about a creative callisthenic: send your character back to school. Of course, if you are writing young adult fiction, they are probably already in school, but you can play around with the idea for other characters as well. Here are some specific school-themed ideas:

1.   Your character must undergo retraining after his/ her job becomes obsolete. What does s/he take? How does s/he feel about this? Who else is in the class: younger students, older students? Does the character form a relationship with another student (not just a love relationship, but also friendships, even mentoring relationships?) Build a story about a character forced to return to school. Explore how that affects his/her life and those of the other students.

2.   Your character decides to take an "enrichment" class for fun. What does s/he take? What happens? How does this affect the other relationships s/he has?

3.   A single mom, empty nester, factory worker, or other "unlikely" student decides to go back to school to become a doctor, lawyer or to get a PhD. Come up with the most unlikely pairing you can think of. For instance, Juanita Carlisle left home at 16 and spent the next 10 years working the streets of the Big City. Through the intervention of a mission ministry, she wants to turn her life around. While cleaning offices at the university, she picks up a brochure about the law school . . . What happens next?

YOU'RE THE VILLAIN

While it is difficult to write believable heroes, it is even more difficult to write a believable and understandable villains. As writers, we are the heroes of our stories. We tell the stories from the hero's perspective and see the world through the hero's eyes. Thus, we empathize with that character and tend to imbue him or her with some of our own traits.

Villains, on the other hand, we keep at arm's length. We may make them interesting, but not always believable, rarely understandable and, hardly ever, sympathetic. Evil characters just emerge in the story, often with no other purpose than to give the hero someone to fight.

Here's an exercise to help make your villains more believable.

Make a list of your own failings. List those moral lapses which tempt you the most (whether you give into them or not). Then write down what you would hope to gain when you fail or are tempted in that way.

For instance, I might write down something like this:

> Greed: I would like to obtain a lot of money so my life would be comfortable, I would be able to buy any luxury I want, and I would be free from the fear of not having enough.

Okay, that gives me a motivation for my character who is holding a kidnap victim for ransom. Maybe, like me, the kidnapper grew up in a working poor family where just keeping food on the table was a challenge. We learned to depend on God, but maybe he was taught to depend on himself, that the world took everything from his family, so he is out to take it back. Now, we have some depth to that character.

Often, the best characters are the ones in whom we see our own faults reflected and magnified.

CHARACTERS AND SETTINGS   53

SICK CHARACTERS

This one came to mind today because—well—I'm sick. I have some aches and pains (more than my usual), and a weird fever that comes and goes. The terrible part about it is that it's bad enough to make me a little bit miserable, but not bad enough for me to feel comfortable curling up in bed all day without feeling guilty.

Anyway, we find out a lot about others and ourselves by the way we handle sickness.

Me? I can be seriously ill, and do what I know is right, stay in bed and take care of myself, and still feel guilty. I tend to try to get back to work too soon and end up getting sicker and missing more time than I would if I had just stayed in bed. If I'm having a tough time with my asthma, and I'm in pain, and I have to go out and deal with people, I have little patience for incompetence or stupidity. These are times when my sister calls me "Ugly Betty."

I prefer to hide away, isolate myself from others and take care of myself. However, if I can't, then I am overly conscious of the burden I'm putting on my caregiver, and I try not to take advantage of it.

Here's the exercise.

Make your character sick. Put him or her in bed with the flu for a week. Write about that character's way of handling getting sick. Write a scene with him/ her interacting with a caregiver.

A variation on this is to give your character a chronic condition like allergies, asthma, a trick knee, carpal tunnel or something else that affects how s/he faces the world.

Okay, I'm going back to bed for a while to feel guilty that I'm not at school (even though today I have no classes, and I'm just missing an office hour). Maybe, I should check in on my online classes.

TAKE YOUR MAIN CHARACTER TO DINNER

Writing short fiction is fairly easy. The plots travel a rather simple route from point A to point B. With longer fiction, things are more complex. It is one thing to have a plot going somewhere, but is that plot consistent with the personality of the character?

When I began to experiment with novel length fiction, my creative flow slowed and then stopped. I needed to know that my plot and my character were consistent. I mentioned this to someone. Their advice: Take your main character to dinner.

Now, when I am stuck, I figure my characters are hungry. I send them to dinner. You can learn a lot about your characters over a meal. Where do they eat? Fancy restaurant or diner? Do they prefer to eat at home? What do they eat? Salads or steak and potatoes? How do they eat? Do they nibble or shovel it in?

At dinner, my characters can review what has happened already in the story. They can talk about what they should do next. Some of these scenes may end up in the finished product, but most of the time they just help me move on to the next scene.

So, if you find yourself stuck, maybe a dinner invitation is in order.

ORGANIZATION AND PLOTTING

What happens next? That is a question that fiction and nonfiction writers alike ask. Whether you plan out each detail of your story or article in advance using a classic outline with Roman numerals and letters, or you just down jot a few ideas on the back of an envelope organization is vital to successful writing. In this chapter we will look at some ideas to improve your fiction plots and nonfiction outlines.

CREATIVE ORGANIZATION

I create a lot of exercises geared toward fiction writing. There is a reason for that. Those type of exercises stretch the creative muscles of all writers. Additionally, "fictional" concepts such as description, characterization and even narrative are useful in nonfiction writing as well. However, today I want to address a concept specific to nonfiction writers: Creative Organization.

Usually, a nonfiction writing assignment suggests an organizational approach. That is fine. I am a big believer in an organic approach to nonfiction organization in which the organization grows naturally from the nature of the topic. Sometimes, though, to move from adequacy to excellency, you need to shake things up and look at an old idea in a new way.

Let's say someone commissions you to write a church history. The classic approach to this type of assignment would be a chronological approach beginning with the church's founding and ending with the current day or even with plans for the future. That certainly is workable, but don't immediately settle for that approach without exploring others.

For instance, if the church has several buildings or wings that have been added on over the years, why not use a spatial approach. Take your reader on a stroll through the church discussing each building, the reasons behind it, the people involved and interesting stories related to the construction.

This is especially good if the release of the history is going to coincide with the opening of a new wing or the start of a new building program. On the other hand, you could take a topical approach and organize by ministries and discuss the histories of each one. Another idea would be to use a "list" approach.

For instance, if your church is celebrating its golden anniversary, you could organize around "milestones." You could call your history "Fifty Milestones in Fifty Years" and choose one milestone per year. You could also choose a thematic approach focusing on a single theme and following that theme throughout the history of the church.

Before settling on a single organizational approach, ask yourself, "Can I handle this more creatively by using an organizational pattern not usually used with this topic?" If you do, you will find that writing nonfiction can be as creative as any other type of writing.

ORGANIZATION AND PLOTTING   57

IMITATE SUCCESS

I spent 15 minutes selling life insurance about 20 years ago. Sales organizations are very big on motivational posters. I remember one which read: "To be successful, imitate success."

This is good advice for writers as well. To learn good writing, study good writers and see what they do to create memorable characters, describe a setting, plot a story, research an article, organize a book, and create an opening and a conclusion. You can do this, by studying their writing. Notice, I said "studying" and not "reading." You read for pleasure, but you study to discover the ways and means that the author uses to tell the story or convey the information.

You can discover many different things by studying the writings of others systematically. In this lesson, let's look at some exercises you can use to discover the "deep structure" of the writing. Deep structure refers to the organization of the article, book, novel, or short story.

Let's say you are thinking about writing a how-to article. If you read a selection of how-to articles, you will notice a structure that usually begins with an engaging hook that and engages the self-interest of the reader, after that is a paragraph explaining how this project is beneficial.

Next, you have the steps, and a conclusion that encourages the reader to do the project.

How do I know this? Well, I've read and outlined several how-to articles. Publishers often prefer a type of deep structure for articles, novels, books and short stories.

These exercises should help you discover that structure:

Article Outlining.

It's not very exciting, but it is a great way to discover the deep structure of an article. Identify the main topics and the subtopics. Do this for several articles and see if you notice a pattern.

Topic Sentence Exercise.

A variation on the article outlining approach is to read an article and copy down the topic sentences for each paragraph. Review several articles. Group the topic sentences under different categories such as: step in process, introduction, establishing benefits, establishes problem, presents solution, component of topic area, etc. See if any patterns jump out at you.

Basic plot outlining.

A traditional fiction plot has 6 components:

Exposition: simply setting the scene,

Action: the initial action that the main character(s) is/ are taking at the beginning of the story,

Conflict: that which interrupts the action,

Complications: this is the rising action portion where several events occur as a result of the conflict which lead to the climax,

Climax: this is the high point of the story the outcome of which will determine the future of the main character. Decisions made here will determine if the outcome is positive or negative, and

Resolution: this is what follows the climax.

Not all stories have an exposition or a resolution. Some begin with the conflict and end with the climax. Others begin at the climax and then tell most of the story in flashback. However, most follow this basic pattern with some minor variations. Jot down notes about each section. What happens in the exposition, what's the conflict, etc.?

ORGANIZATION AND PLOTTING   59

One sentence per chapter.

In studying the deep structure of a book, try this. Read the book and, at the end of each chapter, write one sentence that summarizes the main point of that chapter. In reading fiction, write down one sentence for each chapter that tells what the main character accomplished in that chapter.

I SAW IT IN THE FUNNY PAPERS!

You are planning a short story or a chapter in that best-selling novel, but you find yourself stuck. You just can't see what should happen. Why not draw a comic strip?

Take a sheet of paper and turn it lengthwise. Draw six "frames" on the page. Take out your colored pens, crayons or markers and begin the sketch the scenes in the frames with maybe a note or two underneath as to what is happening. You can add voice "bubbles" over the character's heads if you like. You don't have to be a great artist. Stick figures will work.

After you finish filling up the frames, sit down at the keyboard and write down what you see.

SPECIAL REPORT

I've had a lot of fun with this one working with high school students, but adults get into it as well. The concept is simple. You take a Biblical or historical event and create a special news report for that event.

There are two ways to approach it. My favorite is to treat it as a TV news team "Special Report." The other way is to write a newspaper story about the event. Either way, the idea is to report it from the outside. If it is a Biblical event, this means avoiding "church-ese" and treating it as a secular event.

Just a side note for Sunday School teachers: Kids love this exercise. I've used this with junior high and high school kids as a creative drama exercise.

We've covered Noah building the Ark, The Rapture, and the Resurrection of Christ. I personally produced a radio drama in college based on the rapture in the tradition of Orson Wells' *War of the Worlds* broadcast of the 30s.

STUCK FOR IDEAS? ASK A CHARACTER

You've been writing along, and, suddenly, you hit a point in your story where, regardless of your plot outline, your "snowflake" melts, your "wagon wheel" falls in a pothole, your hero's journey gets detoured, or whatever method you used has failed to tell you where to go next. Ask your characters what they want to accomplish at this very moment.

Sit down and type the question "What is your goal right now?" Then have each of your main characters to answer that question.

For instance, if my main character is a woman who has been trapped in an abusive relationship for years, and her husband has come home drunk and angry just as she is packing her suitcase to leave, you might have the following list of objectives:

> Jane: "I just want to get away from him to safety. But deep in my heart I also want him to love me. I didn't get any love from my father. So, I want to leave, but I also want to stay, but not stay in the situation we have."

> Fred: "I want to keep Jane from leaving. I also want her to know I am in control. I want to feel like I am powerful. I don't want to feel powerless like I did when my dad beat me up as a kid. I want to have love, but I need to be feared. I need her to be exclusively mine. Her whole life needs to revolve around me, or I'm nothing. I need her to respect me."

These answers give you some hints about how the next scene can go. Jane may pause a bit before running for the door. Fred may accuse her of criticizing him among her friends as he takes a swing at her.

ORGANIZATION AND PLOTTING   61

If you have well-defined characters, you have unconsciously given them motivations which will drive their actions. By crafting an imaginary conversation with them, you can use those motivations to refine your plot.

LEAST LIKELY

A story can go stale quickly. Once the reader predicts the next scene, you lose their interest. To keep your writing fresh and interesting you need to continually surprise your reader. One way to do that is to constantly ask yourself the question: "What is least likely?"

You can apply this two ways to your fiction writing. The first is to create unlikely characters. For instance, a classic character in a fantasy novel is a hero taller than everyone else, handsome in every way, muscles rippling and an expert fighter. Why not take it in another direction? Consider having your hero to be a small man, older, a scholar instead of a soldier who wins his battles by cunning instead of brute strength.

Try turning the stereotypes upside down. For instance, classic chick lit has a small town girl move to the big city to find a high powered job, romance and life in the fast lane. Why not have a middle-aged woman move to a small town to find a more leisurely life style?

Plot is another place to look for surprises. Why not ask, when you hit a decision point in your plot, what is the least likely thing my character might do and still remain in character. Maybe your shy character suddenly does something bold. Maybe your fighter tries negotiation instead of fighting.

PATTERNS

I've noticed that most writers are also readers. We usually are inspired to write by what we read. The problem is that as we write, we often find it hard to justify taking time away from writing to read. Well, here's a way to feed your reading fix while advancing your writing skills.

62   CREATIVE CALISTHENICS

Find a book by a writer you respect. After reading a chapter, write down a one-sentence description of each scene in the chapter. No more than one sentence. You would be surprised what you learn about plot, suspense and the general development of a story.

You might discover, for instance, that about every three chapters the author reveals a secret about a different character. You might also notice that emotionally intense chapters are followed by less intense ones. It's not that you are going to try to duplicate that pattern, but you can learn something about successful storytelling which you can apply to your own writing.

THEN THE PHONE RANG

Here's an idea starter for you. "John was jarred awake by the ringing phone. He looked at the clock. 'Who would be calling me at 2 a.m.?' he said as he picked up the phone. On the other end of the line . . ."

You can play around with the time and place. It could be his cell phone ringing. You can use one of the characters in your work-in-progress if you wish. Who is on the other end of the phone? Why are they calling? What is their relationship to the character? How does the character feel about the call?

What does s/he say? How does this phone call change the recipient's life?

A variation on this can be a "block breaker." If you have hit an impasse with your character and the plot, have the phone ring with news that changes everything. You don't have to use it in your final version, but it can be a way of stirring up your creative juices.

THE WORST THING

So, you are writing along or planning your plot (depending on how you write), and, suddenly, you hit a dead end. You don't know what should happen next. Ask yourself, "What's the worst possible thing that could happen now?"

ORGANIZATION AND PLOTTING 63

This works great with action-oriented fiction. The detective has discovered the perfect piece of incriminating evidence, places it in her purse and heads back to her office. On the way back, a purse-snatcher grabs her purse and runs off with it. What does she do now?

It even works with less action-oriented fiction. I'm writing a story about a pastor who has a congregant reveal to him that she is a clone. He is stunned. What's the worst thing that can happen? He handles it poorly. Then, as he is worrying about that, what worse could happen? He gets a call from the president of the church board who has discovered this and has called a board meeting for that night.

In a romance novel, the man and woman find each other and get close. What's the worse thing that can happen? His family will disown him if he gets involved with her, or she finds out he only started going to church to find a wife, or she hears he is already married, or . . .

You get the idea. Remember, a comfortable hero/ heroine makes for a boring story.

WAXING POETIC

Poetry has fallen on hard times recently. This is sad, because the poet speaks directly to the heart of the reader. Even if you do not desire to publish poetry, as a writer it is beneficial to write it. Why? Because poetry teaches you to say a lot in a short space and to touch on raw emotion and wrap it in words. Here are a few exercises to get you started.

POETRY JOURNAL

I have been packing up to move this week. One of the things about moving is that you find all sorts of things that you think you've lost. Tucked behind a bookcase, I found a 30-year-old poetry journal. Actually, it was a Bible study poetry journal. For about two years in my 20s, every night, I read a passage of scripture and wrote a short poem or two based on that scripture.

I got the idea for this from a youth Bible study.

The teacher gave us a Psalm and had us write haiku based on it. It was so powerful. I went home and began to do this with the Psalms. When I finished the Psalms, I went on to Job, Proverbs, Hebrews, a few of the Minor Prophets and Revelation.

This is a wonderful way for busy writers to get in some daily Bible study and hone their writing skills of the same time.

Choose a passage of Scripture, and, instead of just reading it and laying it aside, write a short poem based on it. Write a personal daily devotion. Write a letter to the author (you know who he is) about how that verse or passage of Scripture blessed you.

This doesn't have to be great writing. It just needs to be your heartfelt response to what God has taught you in that Scripture.

For instance, here's what I got out of Psalm 1 v. 1 (December 4, 1976):

> Walking with the ungodly
> The Sinner stopped me
> The Scornful offered me a seat
> God pulled out the chair from under me.

SAY HI TO HAIKU

One time, I casually mentioned to a writing group the power of using haiku writing to study the Bible. Afterward, someone asked me, "Terri, could you tell those of us who don't write poetry how to write haiku?"

There is a short and a long answer to this. I'm going to give you the short answer, but realize that like most art forms the short answer leaves out a lot.

A traditional haiku has three lines with a specific structure. The first and last lines are five syllables long and the middle line is seven syllables long. The last line forms a sort of punch line for the poem.

Traditional Japanese haiku focus on themes from nature. The classic is one that goes:

66   CREATIVE CALISTHENICS

> Frog sits on lily Pad
> Jumps in pond
> Kerplop!

Of course, it doesn't fit the syllable scheme in English. That's one of the nuances of this. The poem still works. The key is the three-line, extremely condensed format. For beginners, the 5-7-5 scheme forces that condensed language on the poet. Also, vital to the poem is the "surprise" in the last line. My first haiku in high school was this:

> A snowball hits me
> I crumple beneath the blow
> Ouch! A Rock! Oh No!

I tried to turn the whole "beautiful nature" theme on its head, but in so doing I was actually true to the haiku form.

Here's one from Psalm 23. The contrast between the first two lines and the darker last line is in keeping with the haiku philosophy.

> Sipping cool water
> Resting in green meadows
> Dark path ahead

Now, try your hand at writing a haiku. How much truth can you squeeze into seventeen syllables?

SENSE POETRY

John Ciardi referred to poetry as "sound and sense." The sound of the words blending with the sensual images takes mere words on a page and turns them into poetry. Here's a little exercise that can help focus your attention on the senses in poetic expression. You might even be able to revise it into a good poem.

Line 1: A one-word title. Choose an emotion for your title like "Hope."

Line 2: Write a four or five word line that expresses that title visually. "Sunrise behind dark clouds"

Line 3: Write a four or five word line that expresses the title through sound. "Birds sing accompanied by the rustle of leaves." (Okay, so it's longer than five words. I got carried away.)

Line 4: Write a four or five word line that expresses the title through the sense of touch. "The weight of a kitten on my lap."

Line 5: Write a four or five word line that expresses the title through taste. "Watermelon juice on my tongue."

Line 6: Write a four or five word line that expresses the title through smell. "The aroma of fresh mown grass."

Line 7: Write a single word which is a type of personal synonym for the title. "Creation."

Your first draft will be awkward, but it should give you some good images to work with.

FOUND POETRY

I used to watch a show called *Junk Yard Wars*. The contestants had one day to build some incredible device out of stuff found in a junk yard. They built things like a catapult, a submarine, a rocket, a street sweeper and a demolition device among other things all out of stuff found in a huge junk yard.

Back in high school English class, we did an exercise called "found poetry." We took phrases found in a newspaper and pieced them together into short freestyle poems in the same way those mechanics built devices out of junk.

I have an updated version of that which I have been playing around with for a few days.

In an effort to elude those nasty spam filters on computers, the junk mail artists have begun to put random words and phrases into the body of the email and then cover them with a picture that contains the message, or they simply put them at the end of the document. I was reading them the other day, and I felt like I was reading some sort of surrealist poetry.

So, I revisited my high school days and wrote some found poetry using them. It was fun, if nonsensical, but a good creative exercise. Here is one of the poems I "wrote" based on a piece of junk email. It's called, "I go do sanity" which was the subject line of the email. It's fun! Try it!

> I go do sanity soured by early disappointment
> Unwilling to damp my good friends' confidence
> When the lookout cried Land-oh
> Amused by her staring at Child-wife
> I resolved to do what I could whether he knew anything of little
> Buried somewhere
> The air of wicked grace
> My former friend, Mr. Universal Application
> Fitted every occurrence of her life
> Like a scarecrow in want of support,
> Other packets had missed me,
> And I had took up his position behind her.

WRITING Rx

Is your plot on life support? Are your characters looking anemic? Do you think your article is succumbing to terminal boredom? Do you suffer from blank screen paralysis? Not to worry. We have a sovereign remedy for what ails your writing. The exercises below should have you up and writing in no time.

ANSWERING YOUR INNER CRITIC

Lack of confidence has defeated more writers than a failing printer. Some of us have sitting on our shoulders or staring at us from the top of the computer, an ugly little critter we'll call "Buster." His job is to try to bust our dreams.

He does this by shouting out things like:

"Who do you think you are that someone should read your article?"

"You, a writer? That's a laugh!""Nobody wants to read what you write"

"People will laugh at you,"

"You're writing stinks. Go back to knitting."

Well, if Buster is going to talk to you, you might as well talk to him. You aren't getting any writing done anyway. Write a dialogue between you and Buster. Set the scene. Where you are going to meet him? My own personal image is out on some windswept prairie with the tumbleweeds blowing by, and we are slowly marching toward each other.

Now, let Buster speak. Let him tell you all the things that keep you from writing, that make you feel worthless, that make you feel like you are wasting your time, or that make you feel like you lost whatever talent you had, or that people will look at you funny if you say you are a writer, or whatever it is that Buster throws at you.

Then respond. Tell him off. Tell him why it doesn't matter if what you wrote yesterday wasn't that good because you are going to rewrite it today. Tell him that you are worthy because you are a Child of God. Tell him that it doesn't matter what people think. Be prepared, though, he probably has some comebacks. Write those down too and then respond. Keep the dialog going until you defeat him? Well, at least for that day. The worst thing that can happen is you spend several minutes writing, and anything that gets you writing is a good thing.

A NEW PERSPECTIVE

We all know that the perspective from which a story is written is important. Even if you have chosen your POV for a story, it doesn't hurt to examine the same story from a variety of points of view. Kahil Gibran's *Jesus of Nazareth* tells the story of Christ through the eyes of a score of people who might have known him. It adds depth to the gospel story seeing the life of Christ through so many eyes.

Learning to write creatively is important for nonfiction writers as well. Writing about an event that happened to you for a devotional or an anthology is much like fiction writing.

You probably tell the story from your own point of view (I don't mean just first person here, but rather as a focus on the event from a particular person's perspective). You might write in the first person about something your son did. You can tell that from your point of view: what you did, how it affected you, your interpretation of it, or you could write it from his—how he saw the events, how he felt about it, etc.

Even writing how-tos can be affected by imagining yourself as a typical reader and writing a letter to the editor about how you used the information in the article. Here are a few specific exercises to help you experience different points of view:

Letters.

Take an event in your story. Have each of the characters write someone about that event. What happened from their perspective? What did they think about it? What was their perspective? You can even have a bystander or extremely minor character write about it. A variation on this is to write a diary or journal entry.

Observation.

Go to a public event such as a play, concert, church service, or sporting event. Watch what happens. Make some notes. When you get home, write about what happened from at least three perspectives. You can even imagine the thoughts of the people. Write in the first person, if that helps you. For instance, after attending a church service, you could write about it from the points of view of the pastor, the choir director, a person in the pew, and the little kid who was squirming all through service.

Your Story, Different Storyteller.

Describe something dramatic that happened to you from a different POV. For instance, most of us write personal experiences in the first person. Try writing it in the third. You could even write it in the second person. Assume you had amnesia as the main character, and someone else is telling you what happened.

BEAT THE CLOCK

Back in the early days of television, there was a game show called *Beat the Clock*. Contestants were given weird assignments like having to carry five balloons on a spoon across the stage in 30 seconds. They won points for exceeding the goal. I was watching an old rerun of this show in the wee hours of the morning on the Game Show Channel and thought, "That's a great idea for writers who have trouble turning off the inner critic on the first draft." So, here's my version of *Beat the Clock*.

First, you need to set a base line. Take your work in progress or some other project and write as you normally would for fifteen minutes. Count the number of words you wrote. For instance, I normally write about 1000 words an hour (four double-spaced type written pages) at rough draft speed. So, I would put down 250 words as a base line.

Second, set a goal of five percent above your base line. For me, that would be 12.5 words. Let's be generous and round it down to 12. So, my goal will be 262 words.

Finally, set a timer for 15 minutes and write trying to meet or beat that goal. If you do, give yourself a cookie or some other reward. If not, take one word off and try again.

A variation on this is to do it with a friend. Whoever beats their personal goal by more words buys the smoothies the next time you are in Jamba Juice. (I don't drink coffee, but you could use Starbucks instead, I guess.)

Remember, the idea of first drafts is to simply get the basic ideas down in writing. It is not to have a perfect or even good piece of writing. That all comes in the editing process. Games like this will help you turn off the inner critic and just write on that first draft.

CUT IT IN HALF

You and I are writers. That means we love words. Big words, little words, exotic words, and words that taste good in your mouth while you say them, words that you chew on and digest with the gusto of a starving man at a banquet table. We love them all. In fact, we love them too much, and, just like that earlier sentence, our writing gets—well—wordy. Here's an exercise for those of us too much in love with words.

Take something you have written. It can be a story, a chapter, an article or essay. Be sure it is at least 1500 words. Set a timer or alarm clock for one hour. In that hour, cut the piece of writing in half. The writing still has to make sense. Nevertheless, take out everything you can. Here is a list to guide you:

Take out all adverbs. Most are unnecessary.

Take out all redundancies. Doors always bang LOUDLY and never softly. Fires are always hot, so why say, "Hot fire."

Reduce adjective clutter. Cut out all you can.

Remove any paragraphs, quotes, statistics or facts from an article that do not support the theme of the article.

Remove your weakest paragraph or main point. In any nonfiction article, there is usually one main point that is not as well supported or as interesting as the others are. Get rid of it.

Ask how much physical description you need in a scene. Get rid of what is not essential. (Note: I said essential when I was thinking "absolutely necessary.")

To make this more fun, do it with a writing friend. Set a timer and see who can cut their piece most?

BEATING THE BLOCK

Most of us face writers block at one time or another. We sit staring at the computer screen, our fingers hovering over the keys, seemingly suspended in space wondering what to write. Here are a few ways to beat the block:

Word Association.

Sometimes, if I'm slow to start, I'll play the word association game. The way it works is that I type a key word relevant to the topic of the article or scene in a story. Then, I write down the first word that comes to mind after seeing that word. After that, I write down a word suggested by the second word, and so on, until I start writing phrases and sentences and come unblocked.

The Dramatic Quote.

Write down the most dramatic quote you found in your research. Use this quote as your lead and ask, "What comes next?" Even if you don't use the quote as your lead in the final draft, it can get you writing.

Understand the Block.

Resistance always has meaning. One way to approach writer's block is to find the meaning behind it. Open a new document file or take out a notebook and begin to "interview" yourself. Ask, "What am I afraid will happen if I write something?"

Very often, our fears keep us from being truly creative. We have those voices of others who laughed at our dreams of writing, belittled it, or patronized us when we brought it up. Maybe we believe that what we write will be "wrong." Maybe we are afraid of the responsibility of people reading our words and taking action because of them. Once you understand what those fears are, ask yourself, "Are these fears real; if so, are they significant?"

Write about the Block.

Just begin to write about being blocked. Stay "in the now" and write, "Okay, I'm sitting at the keyboard. I don't have anything to say. I've got writers block. I wonder why they call it a block. Is it wooden and square with a letter on the side of it? I liked playing with blocks as a kid . . ."

Diversion.

The more you think about the block the more blocked you will become. Therefore, one good way to beat the block is to do something entirely different from writing. Physical exercise or doing mundane chores make good diversions. Work out, take a walk, mow the lawn, do the dishes, or vacuum the floor. Don't think about the story or writing at all. That way you can come back to the writing with a fresh perspective.

Relaxation.

One way to overcome writer's block is to simply lie down on a couch and clear your mind. One good way to do this is to imagine a peaceful scene. It could be an ocean shore, a meadow, a woods or mountaintop. It doesn't matter as long as it is peaceful to you. Soft music can help as well as relaxation tapes.

Switch Writing Instruments.

Each of us composes our manuscripts in different ways. Some writers like to write out the articles long hand and then transcribe them on the computer. Others, like myself, compose at the keyboard. If you compose with pencil and paper, try using the computer. If you compose at a keyboard, try writing long hand. Sometimes switching writing instruments will be enough to shake loose those creative cobwebs. Sometimes, I'll switch between typing on the keyboard to using voice recognition software. Hearing the sound of my voice can be enough to give me a fresh perspective on what I'm writing.

76   CREATIVE CALISTHENICS

BEYOND THE VISUAL

When I teach writing, I notice my students think about description as being primarily visual. Occasionally, they will include a sound or two. However, to read their writings, one would think that human beings only had two senses: sight and sound. Touch, taste and smell trigger some of the most powerful sense memories. You need to let your reader do more than see and hear; you need to impact their other three senses. Here are a few exercises to help you think more creatively.

1. Go back over a piece of description you have already written. Count the number of references by sense. For instance: Sight 15, sound four, smell 0, taste 0, and touch 2. Rewrite the piece trying to bring in any senses you missed. Taste is often the most challenging. Nevertheless, think about creative ways to include it. For instance, you could indicate a man is nervous by pointing out his perspiration with a bit of visual description. On the other hand, you could simply have him lick his lips and taste the saltiness of the sweat on his upper lip. Don't worry about it sounding forced. This is just an exercise. You can revise or eliminate anything that doesn't work before your final draft.

2. Pretend you are Helen Keller. Go to a location and imagine that Ann Sullivan has left you to sit here while she went to the bathroom. Describe the scene without using sight or sound references.

3. Smells are particularly powerful in evoking emotion. Make a list of smells that evoke some sort of feeling in you. Here's mine:

•Fresh cut grass on a summer afternoon reminds me of childhood in a small town.

•The musty smell of paper and old leather in a used bookstore as I open a century-old book. It smells like history in my hands.

♦The tangy, sweet, wet smell of an orange being peeled makes my mouth water.

♦The antiseptic smell of Lysol reminds me of hospitals and last illnesses and worry.

♦The smoky smell of bacon: My Mom making BLTs on Sunday evening after church. A warm family feeling.

Well you get the idea. Don't handicap your characters, let them see and hear, but have them smell, taste and feel as well.

HEAR THE WORDS

I've been writing a training course for new online teachers. One of the things we must cover is making sure that web resources are accessible to visually-impaired students using a screen reader. Unfortunately, sighted individuals create graphic-intensive, tables-driven web sites without considering the problems those cause for visually-impaired visitors to the web sites. I tend to be conscious of such things because my mother was visually impaired.

To make sure my sites were accessible, I downloaded Thunder, a screen reader program that comes packaged with WebbIE, a text-based web browser, to test out the materials I am using. On a lark, and because my eyes were getting a little blurry after about four hours online, I decided to listen to my work-in-progress. It was amazing what I caught listening to the words. I've edited by reading aloud for years, but to hear it read, really helped me pick up on awkward phrases, grammatical issues and missed plurals, even misspelled words the spell checker didn't catch.

The software is free. You can get it at http://www.screenreader.net

78   CREATIVE CALISTHENICS

TWENTY-FIVE WORDS OR LESS

Many pieces of writing simply lack focus. Here's an exercise you can use to help refine your focus. For one of your works-in-progress, do the following. Write down what the story, article, essay, book or novel is about in 25 words or less. It's a simple exercise, but it is not so simple to do.

Here are a few literary examples:

Pilgrims Progress: A man journeys from the city of destruction to the celestial city combating obstacles along the way.

Huckleberry Finn: In the antebellum south, a boy runs away from home on a raft and helps a slave escape to the north.

Hamlet: A young man, who discovers his mother and uncle killed his father and married each other, seeks revenge.

Now, add your story to the list.

VIDEO CAMERA

We have all heard the advice to "show, not tell" in our writing. However, it's just so much easier to say, "Jane felt sad about the loss of her child" than to find some way to show that sadness to an audience.

What you need is a change of perspective. Imagine you are not a writer privy to the inner thoughts of your characters. Instead, you are video camera following her around. You simply describe what you see. Please, don't cheat by saying, "she looked sad" or "she had a sad look in her eyes." What does sadness in the eyes actually look like? In fact, get rid of all labels for emotions like sad, happy, angry, bitter, worried, etc. Just stick to what a video camera sees. Maybe something like this:

> "Jane walks into the room. She pauses as she opens the door. The crib stands at one end of the room. She approaches it. She caresses the wood. She picks up a picture of a baby. She slumps into the antique rocker beside the crib and begins to cry."

This is what the camera would see. I used no emotional labels. I showed what happened, and I let you interpret those actions.

So, if you find that you are telling more than showing, stop writing and start videoing.

WRITE A BAD STORY

There is a competition every year for writing the worst story. The story begins with "It was a dark and stormy night . . ." (Remember, that's how Snoopy begins his story in the Peanuts comic script.) The idea is to use every cliché, every cardboard, stereotypical character and create the story that is so bad it's good.

Well, I do something similar with my speech students. I have them give a terrible speech. My favorite was the girl who pretended to be a drunk giving a speech at an AA meeting.

Anyway, it's a fun exercise. Start writing something in your favorite genre (fiction, nonfiction, poetry, reportage, etc.) and do everything wrong. Fill it with redundant adverbs and adjectives, use weak passive tense, use clichés and stereotyped characters, use long, pretentious words instead of simple language, be wordy, abstract, and vague. Tell, don't show. And don't forget to add the "tacked on moral" at the end.

CHANGE OF SCENE

While it is generally a good idea to write in the same place everyday so you begin to associate the creative process with that place, it is also good to break away from the desk or kitchen table. Here's an exercise to get you out of the house and, at the same time, hone your descriptive skills.

Take a pad and a pen or your laptop and go somewhere real. It can be the ocean, a park, a restaurant, the mall, an airport or anywhere where you can set and watch the drama of life unfold before you.

Simply sit and write a description of what you experience there. Describe the scene using at least four out of five senses. Use all five if there is any way to add taste to the mix realistically. You can describe the scene as if it were static and create a word picture. If you are daring, focus on the action and follow one particular character as if you were following her or him with a video camera and describe the scene in the present tense.

GAMES
AND
COLLABORATIONS

*Writing tends to be a solitary pursuit. The writer works all alone develop-
ing his or her skills. However, sometimes it is fun to develop those skills
along with others. Participation in critique groups and writer's associa-
tions are two good ways to add a social dimension to your writing. These
exercises suggest a few others.*

WORD WARS

One of the biggest problems I have is turning off the inner critic during my
first draft. I'm guessing you have the same problem. However, it must be
done. This is vital for two reasons. First, composing and editing represent different brain functions. Switching back and forth between them slows down
the creative flow. Secondly, because of this frequent switching, you find yourself stuck for what to write next. Often, so-called "Writer's Block" results
from intimidation by your inner critic.

82   CREATIVE CALISTHENICS

Here's a fun way to kick start your creativity and put your critic in a holding cell until you need her on the next draft. You need a writing buddy for this one. You can do this while physically together or use the internet for communication. Choose someone evenly matched with you so you don't feel intimidated by someone with more experience.

Set a time period for writing together. The time frame doesn't really matter much. It can be a day, an hour or, my favorite, 15-30 minutes. The object of the game is simple: write more words in that time frame than your friend. You can raise the stakes by creating an incentive like the one who loses buys the coffee the next time you go out.

"TAG, YOU'RE IT!"

I had my first experience with this exercise in a high school typing class. The teacher had each of us write a single paragraph of a story then move one typewriter to the left and continue the story that student had started. We continued that way around the room and then read each of the stories aloud. You can do the same thing with email. Here's how it works.

Harry, Martha, Linda and Tom want to have some fun writing. Harry begins by writing a paragraph or two of a story. He emails it to the list and "tags" someone to continue. At the end of his post, he writes, "Tag Martha, you're it." Martha picks up the story and "tags" someone else. They continue this way until they get tired of the story, or someone writes an ending.

The results can be hilarious, and it is good mental exercise having to adapt to unexpected changes in the storyline.

GAMES AND COLLABORATIONS   83

ALL A-TWITTER

Okay, I succumbed. I just signed up for Twitter (http://www.twitter.com/terrimain). Twitter is a social networking program on which you can post very short notes of 140 characters answering the question, "What are you doing now?" I'm not sure how useful it will be for me. I have a feeling that, if I was 15, I'd be "Tweeting" my friends all the time. After turning those numbers around and adding a few, I'm not so sure. But it got me thinking about a bunch of Twitter exercises.

Character Tweets.

Send out Tweets (posts on Twitter are called Tweets) about what your character is doing right now. For instance, in my work-in-progress, I might write: "Carolyn and Mike get Amanda out of jail and learn that Kim might have known Juan at O'neill space habitat." Even if you don't use Twitter, you can pretend your character sent you a Tweet. "Whew! Arresting Amanda what did they think? Got to talk to Kim. She knew Juan before."

Tweet Pitches.

We are often too wordy when sending off a query or a proposal. We wander around never getting to the essence of the pitch. Imagine a publisher/editor is on the other end and do a 140 character pitch. "Two professors on the moon investigate a murder, save the planet and fall in love." Or for nonfiction "Shyness affects many, but it can be overcome."

Tweet Scenes.

Try putting out a series of Tweets describing the next four or five scenes in your book. For non-fiction writers, do the same thing with chapters or sub-sections of your chapter.

Tweet Fiction.

I just recently heard about this. Some people are composing the ultimate flash fiction. I haven't tried it yet, but it might be a fun exercise to try to get conflict, crisis and resolution into 140 characters. A variation on this is to put out a series of Tweets which link together to form a story.

THE PICTURE GAME

This exercise helps you develop your observation and description skills. It is a game which requires two people.

One person is the writer, and the other is the artist. Find a painting in an art book or a photograph and write a detailed description of the picture. When you are finished, hand the description to your partner, the artist (who has been writing a description of a picture for you). Using colored pens, try to recreate the picture from that person's description. Compare the results with the picture. How close did you come (given your artistic skill set) to replicating the picture from the word description alone?

This is also a good exercise for a writing class or writer's group.

GET A (SECOND) LIFE

I was just over in Second Life. (http://www.secondlife.com) It's a virtual world where you can build houses, hold meetings, take classes, buy stuff, and just hang out with virtual friends. It's kind of neat because you can fly there too. Some of these people really get into building, and they have a bunch beautiful art galleries and replicas of famous buildings that you can "walk around in." I saw a wonderful replica of the Sistine Chapel the other day. It's as close to the real thing as I'm going to get. There are also churches, Bible studies, support groups, one minister even has a "rescue mission" in one of the -er- more colorful parts of SL.

GAMES AND COLLABORATIONS 85

Anyway, here's an exercise if you like hanging out in virtual worlds like Second Life or even World of Warcraft (I'll pray for you). Take time to go to a public area with lots of people and just sit back and observe. Take notes. Build stories about the avatars. Where does that one with the wings fly? What does she see? What adventures might she have? What about that guy building a rocket in the sandbox (a public place for building things)? Where does he plan to go with it? Visit some of the historical sims, (sim=region of SL) and place a story in that sim.

Imagine the people behind the avatars. I stay pretty close to my own hair color and height. I'm a bit more slender in SL, and my hair stays in place better, but it's close to my own appearance. Some people go to extremes, though. That muscle-bound avatar may be a 98-pound weakling at home.

Membership in Second Life is free. If you want to hang out there and do some observing and writing, it can be fun. I have a place there. My username is Terri Marathon. If you are in-world, instant message me, and I'll teleport you to my new place—a Tudor-style cottage/ manor house. I'm still decorating, but I can send you a landmark and we can visit.

Terri Main teaches communication studies at Reedley College in Reedley, California, where she lives with her cats Patches, Fluffy, and Inkspot. She has been writing professionally for more than forty years and teaching students to write for more than thirty. She is editor of WayfarersJournal.com, an online science fiction magazine. She has published magazine articles in a variety of publications including Woman's World, Income Opportunities, Writer's Digest, American Way, Kiwanis and Sunday Woman. She also consults on marketing for writers.

To get a weekly Creative Calisthenics writing tip, visit the website at www.creativecalisthenics.com and click on "Weekly Tip."

Get big creativity tips, writing prompts and exercises for your imagination throughout the week from Creative Calisthenics at Twitter: www.twitter.com/creativeworkout

If you're on Facebook, The Creative Calisthenics group URL is: www.facebook.com/pages/ CreativeCalisthenics/135644124037

Recommended Manuscript Evaluation Services

www.TheFinishers.biz

Award-winning novelist Frank Creed, from The Finishers, provides critiques, evaluations, and mentorship programs that will release the magic in your writing. Visit www.thefinishers.biz for details.

"I have been writing and teaching writing for nearly 30 years and have set under some of the best writing teachers on the West Coast. Nevertheless, Frank Creed taught me a new way of looking at my writing and took it to the next level. His critiques soared above my graduate school evaluations in their completeness and practical help. Frank's approach is detailed, direct and immediately applicable. He not only helps you finish the manuscript at hand, but gives you tools to improve your writing overall whether you are a beginner or an old pro."
—Terri Main

Breinigsville, PA USA
12 August 2010
243515BV00001B/3/P